GHOST HUNTING

Secrets of the Supernatural

Discover ghosts across the country—and in your own backyard—with paranormal investigators Amy Bruni and Adam Berry.

CONTENTS

FORT KNOX IN PROSPECT, MAINE
Join Amy and Adam, as well as some ghostly soldiers, inside the thick walls of this historic garrison on page 62.

Amy and Adam, along with paranormal researcher and historian John Tenney, set up in the Villisca Ax Murder House. Go to page 18 to see how their investigation turned out.

Foreword

YOUR PARANORMAL ADVENTURE

Amy Bruni and Adam Berry aren't just colleagues, they're best friends. Their close connection has helped them explore haunted locations, hunt down famous ghosts and get it all on camera for their show *Kindred Spirits*. Now they're sharing their experiences and unique methods for investigations to help others conduct paranormal research of their own.

As told to Gina McIntyre

THERE'S A REASON WE CHOSE THE title *Kindred Spirits* for our series. It speaks not only to our incredibly close friendship but also to our shared approach to paranormal investigation. When we travel to haunted places, we set out to truly communicate with the people—living and dead—at every location, and that humane and honest method has yielded exciting results. Since we embarked on this path—first as curious amateurs, now as seasoned professionals—our lives have been enriched in ways we could never have imagined. Quite honestly, every day brings a new and welcome sense of adventure.

Modern-day ghost hunting, of course, has its roots in the most enduring traditions in history. Telling ghost stories around the campfire, pondering life's unknowable, unanswerable mysteries—these are things that have always occupied the corners of the human imagination. We feel so fortunate to spend our time pursuing a vocation that connects us to the past, enlightens our present and informs our attitudes about what might come to pass when we finally cross over into the next world.

It also brings us so much joy. Since starting out on the paranormal circuit, we've traversed the country many times over, visiting the most far-flung reaches of the United States. We've seen some of the most beautiful natural landscapes, some of the most breathtaking architecture and some of the most unsettling reminders of the darker chapters of our collective history. These are experiences we wouldn't trade for the world.

In this issue, we recount some of our most memorable interactions with the people and entities—some kindly, others less so—we've met along the way. We're grateful to share the benefit of our years out in the field to inspire a new generation of investigators to hit the road. You don't have to venture far from home to expand your horizons in surprising ways, we promise.

But for those of you with a bit more wanderlust in your hearts, embrace that curiosity, that hunger to know more, and let it be your guide. Go out and learn all you can about the people—living and not—who shape your community, your country and the world at large. It's sure to be a thrilling, consciousness-expanding trip. Just always be sure to lead with compassion—in paranormal interactions and in life.

Happy haunting!
Amy Bruni and Adam Berry

What strange noises have gotten you out of bed in the darkest hours?

THINGS THAT GO BUMP IN THE NIGHT

Since the dawn of time, people have been telling stories about unexplained sights and sounds—the things that wake you up in the wee hours and keep you from going back to sleep.

By Julie Tremaine

SOME OF LIFE'S BIGGEST questions have haunted us since the dawn of mankind: Why are we here? What does it all mean? And what happens when we die? The short answer is that we all have our own personal beliefs, and for many people, that's enough. But the longer answer, the one that pushes the search for meaning beyond the boundaries of our known world, is far more complicated.

Fascination with the paranormal—that is, things beyond the scope of normal scientific understanding—is as old as human history itself. Creating stories about beings placed in the sky by the gods, what we now call constellations, reaches all the way back to prehistoric cultures in the Paleolithic and Neolithic periods. And really, what are legends about ancient, unknowable beings other than predecessors to ghost stories? Tales of what lies beyond our understanding have circulated for millennia. People in ancient Egypt, in ancient Greece, in China and in India all told each other ghost stories. The *Epic of Gilgamesh*, a poem that dates back to the seventh century BCE, offers a description of the afterlife.

Around the same time in ancient China, there were such strong beliefs in the power of spirits over people's lives that they wrote contracts purchasing land from the spirits so they could safely bury their relatives. The contract would be buried with the person, and paper symbolizing money would be burned at the burial site to represent finalizing the transaction.

There are even ghost stories in the Bible, like in the first Book of Samuel when Saul consults a medium to communicate with the spirit of Samuel. In the Book of

Are ancient myths about gods and constellations rooted in ghost stories?

John, Jesus resurrects Lazarus, a man who has been entombed for four days and returns from the dead.

In ancient Rome, they told one another ghost stories as an attempt to understand what lies beyond our basic comprehension. Pliny the Younger, a Roman author and judge from the first and second century CE, philosophized about ghosts in a letter that has survived to this day, in which he asks the friend to whom he's writing whether he believes in ghosts. Pliny then went on to recount a story that "particularly inclines me to give credit to their existence" about a woman "of a size and beauty more than human" who made predictions about a man's future, all of which came true.

WHY DO PEOPLE LOOK FOR GHOSTS?

As civilizations progressed and the world grew more connected, it became increasingly common to consult spirit mediums and those who believe they can see or communicate with the dead. In the Victorian era, séance parties were the height of fashion. Not so long after, tarot card readers and fortune tellers—or those who claimed to be, at least—would travel from town to town with carnivals.

So while ghost hunting as we know it today is a relatively new practice, the search for the meaning of ghosts and the desire to uncover the unknown forces in our lives is as ancient as our species. In fact, according to a 2005 Gallup poll, some three-quarters of Americans believe in some form of the paranormal. About one in three Americans, according to the Pew Research Center in 2015, believe that they've made some kind of contact with the

People have long gone to fortune-tellers in hopes of getting messages from the dead.

FREQUENTLY ASKED QUESTIONS

Are Curses Real?

Curses, both ancient and modern, have been part of the conversation about the supernatural since ancient times. For example, the Egyptian "mummy's curse," which said that misfortune would befall anyone who disturbed a pharaoh's tomb, gained so much traction after King Tutankhamun's tomb was discovered that the curse was even blamed for the deaths of a number of those involved in the excavation. Stories and legends of misfortune and untimely deaths during productions of Shakespeare's *Macbeth* have surrounded the play for so long that thespians only refer to it as "that Scottish play" inside theatres. Not so long ago, legions of sports fans put credence in the Curse of the Bambino, which meant that after trading Babe Ruth to the New York Yankees in 1920, the Boston Red Sox couldn't win a World Series. "The curse was reversed," as fans commonly say, in 2004. The same allegedly occurred with the Chicago Cubs, which last won a World Series in 1908. The Billy Goat Curse started when Billy Goat Tavern owner William Sianis wasn't allowed to bring his pet goat, Murphy, into a Cubs game in the 1945 World Series. He damned the team, and they didn't win another series until 2016.

"Most people these days surely don't believe in supernatural curses," wrote Ken Drinkwater, senior lecturer and researcher in cognitive and parapsychology, and Neil Dagnall, reader in applied cognitive psychology, both of Manchester Metropolitan University, for the independent news site *The Conversation*. "But their prevalence in the media suggests that they still have a hold on psyches, and that a good amount of people still pay credence to them." Simply put: a curse is the kind of thing that becomes more real the more energy you invest in it. If you believe a curse is real, you'll inherently—and unconsciously—look for evidence to support that belief.

"Believers in curses may look for affirming evidence, such as potentially related bad luck, and discount contradictory data," Drinkwater and Dagnall write. "This confirmatory bias produces coherent, but logically inconsistent narratives supporting the presumption of supernatural forces." So no, you're probably not cursed because you cheated at a board game when you were eight—but you also probably shouldn't go unearthing tombs in the Valley of the Kings, either. Wouldn't want to invite any unwelcome attention from an ancient Egyptian pharaoh, right?

dead, and at least one in five claim to have seen a ghost.

Any paranormal investigator will tell you that they started looking for things that go bump in the night because, at the most basic level, it's fun. But for many people, it morphs into more than that. Both Amy Bruni and Adam Berry started out as people who had an interest in the paranormal, who then found like-minded people in amateur investigating groups. As their passion for the topic grew, so did their involvement in the larger paranormal community.

Now, their main goal in searching for ghosts is to find people who need help—whether living or dead—and give them the assistance they need. One of the most common messages the two get from entities is "help me." Often, a spirit will have stayed behind for a reason. Whether they've chosen to be there, or they need to convey a message, or finish something that requires someone living to help (or even just listen) means the entity isn't finished with this plane yet. On their television show, *Kindred Spirits*, the two try to help ghosts get enough closure to move on or find peace.

"Belief in ghosts has soared in recent decades, from one in ten Americans to one in three," wrote Claude Fischer, sociology professor at the University of California, for the school's *Berkeley Blog* in 2013. "Moreover, young Americans are about twice as likely as old Americans to say they have consulted psychics, believe in ghosts, and believe in haunted houses. . . . It's a magical nation. And that goes back a long time."

But really, we are no closer to understanding what ghosts are today than we were 2,000 years ago. Despite all of our scientific advances, and a world more connected than ever that allows the para-curious to share information and resources, the paranormal is still a field that is passionately studied and keenly observed but never conclusively explained.

Some might say that's half the fun of looking for ghosts in the first place.

As new ghost hunters quickly discover, there are many ways to explore the paranormal—and not all of them involve sitting in creepy old basements in the middle of the night. You just have to love pushing the boundaries of your own knowledge and searching for answers in unexpected places. The beauty of this kind of work is that you can choose exactly what kind of weirdness you want to learn about. There are so many strange and spooky paths to go down.

WHAT EXACTLY ARE GHOSTS?

Technology has advanced to allow ghost hunters to capture phenomenon previously limited to one's memory. It can be used to enhance ordinary human perception. But what exactly is that tech capturing? Some people believe that ghosts are manifestations of our own emotions, while others will say that when we see ghosts, we're really seeing our subconscious thoughts coming to light. In some religions, ghosts are explained as a soul without a body. Skeptics, of course, will say that they aren't real at all. While there are many different definitions of what a ghost is (or isn't), the one that's most commonly accepted is that

Some people believe ghosts can manifest as orbs of light.

Mold and drafts in old buildings account for a lot of events that seem paranormal but aren't.

Spirits may remain in places that were important to them in life or where their bodies were laid to rest.

a ghost or spirit is an energetic being that stays behind after a person's death.

Ghosts can manifest as full- or partial-body apparitions, or sometimes as orbs of light, but sometimes they don't appear visibly at all. Often, a spirit's energy can be perceived by equipment but not by the naked eye. It's possible for a ghost to make its presence known in many other ways, like speaking aloud, knocking on things or making other noises, or moving objects. Sometimes, a spirit can even change the temperature in a space.

When a ghost like this is present in a space, it's referred to as an active haunting. It's the presence of a person who has chosen to be there. Those spirits are the ones Amy and Adam investigate on *Kindred Spirits*.

Sometimes, especially in cases of traumatic deaths, a spirit's essence can imprint on one specific space, and create a residual haunting. Unlike an active haunting, this energy clings to a space, and will often repeat the same behavior over and over. In a case like this, no amount of conversation can help. It's almost as though the moment is frozen in time.

ARE GHOSTS REAL?

Ghosts are real if you believe they are. There is no solid evidence of spirits, no scientific measurements to quantify or define what is or isn't a ghost. In fact, quite the opposite. Science has been trying to disprove the paranormal—to provide what skeptics perceive as rational explanations—as to why people believe they experience spooky experiences. But those explanations have fallen short of fully explaining many people's experiences.

Scientific American, when examining science-based explanations for paranormal experiences, offered possible causes like low-frequency sounds as the cause of feelings of unease or nervousness. "Exposure to mold is known to cause neurologic symptoms like delirium, dementia, or irrational fears," astrophysicist Sabrina Stierwalt, PhD, wrote for the website in 2019. "So is it a coincidence that the houses we suspect are haunted also tend to be in disrepair and so quite possibly full of toxic mold?" Carbon monoxide, she added, can cause hallucinations, and drafts often explain slamming doors or objects moving.

Skepticism is important in an investigation, and the things Dr. Stierwalt lists are all important to check for in investigating a space for paranormal activity. In fact, more often than not, you'll likely find a non-paranormal answer for what you think might be paranormal activity in a space. There have been many times that Amy and Adam have explained strange activity by finding tangible reasons for it, from mold and carbon monoxide to high levels of electromagnetic frequency that can affect brain function.

Believing in a brush with the supernatural can be amplified if it was a shared experience, added Stierwalt. "We are more likely to believe in a paranormal experience if someone else who was there can back up our belief," she wrote. "So while we might be able to convince ourselves that we were somehow mistaken about what we saw or heard, we tend to put more stock into someone else's eyewitness account if it also backs our suspicions."

But if you've had a brush with the paranormal, you know that it's difficult to deny something out of the ordinary has happened. Even if that experience wasn't captured

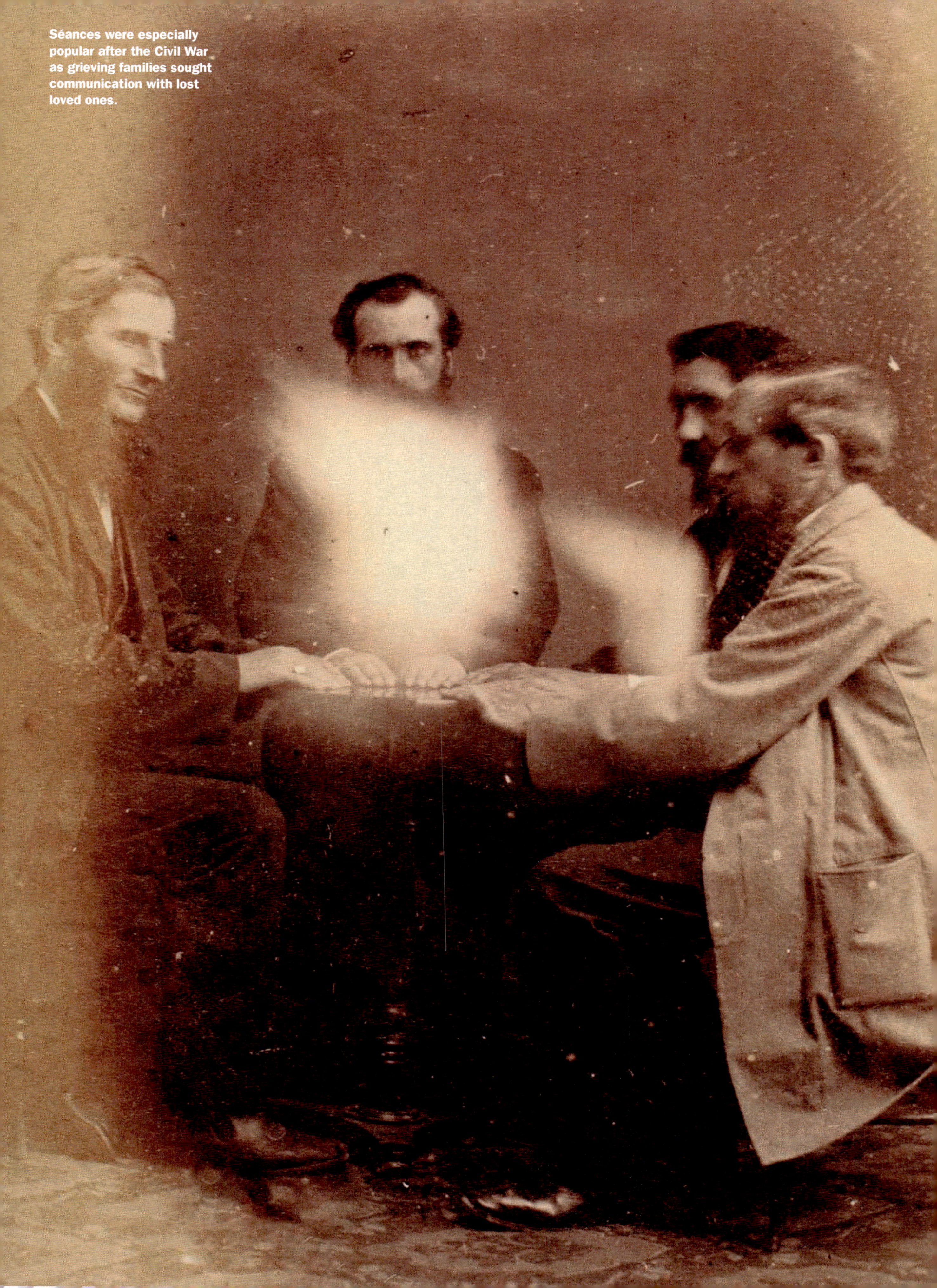

Séances were especially popular after the Civil War as grieving families sought communication with lost loved ones.

FREQUENTLY ASKED QUESTIONS

How to Address a Ghost

The short answer? Exactly like you'd speak to anyone else. David Robson, in an article for BBC Future, relayed an anecdote about two of the world's most famous leaders. "Soon after World War II, Winston Churchill was visiting the White House when he is said to have had an uncanny experience," Robson wrote. "Having had a long bath with a Scotch and cigar, he reportedly walked into the adjoining bedroom—only to be met by the ghost of Abraham Lincoln. Unflappable, even while completely naked, Churchill apparently announced: 'Good evening, Mr. President. You seem to have me at a disadvantage.' The spirit smiled and vanished." Did Churchill *really* see Lincoln? We'll never know for sure—but the anecdote, regardless of our ability to prove it, relays a valuable lesson in how to speak to ghosts: with respect.

on video or in an audio recording, if it was meaningful or important to you, isn't that enough?

IT'S THE PERFECT TIME TO LOOK FOR ANSWERS

In times of great distress, people tend to search for answers anywhere they can find them—and after large, life-altering events, like the COVID-19 pandemic, people have historically turned to the paranormal.

After the Civil War ended in 1865, bereaved families in search of closure turned to séances and other ways to connect with their deceased loved ones. The idea became so popular and widespread that it gave rise to the Spiritualist movement, when Victorian séance parties became the height of fashion. "Spiritualism was popular," according to the BBC, "not just because it could entertain and provide comfort to the believer, but also because it seemed to combine the empirical methods and discoveries of science (such as the invisible force of electricity) with the religious idea of the afterlife."

During and after the Vietnam War, a number of paranormal researchers rose to international prominence, such as Ed and Lorraine Warren, who famously investigated the homes and families on which *The Conjuring* and *Annabelle* are based, and Hans Holzer, who did the same with the family and home that later became *The Amityville Horror*. In times of intense stress and emotional strain, people tend to perceive more paranormal activity and to search for explanations for it.

This could be linked to what *Psychology Today* calls "the sensed presence," a feeling of not being alone in difficult times. "The sensed presence usually happens to individuals who have become isolated in an extreme or unusual environment, often when high levels of stress are involved," Frank McAndrew, PhD, a professor of psychology at Knox College, wrote for the magazine in 2015. "These individuals report a perception or feeling that another person is there to help them cope with a hazardous situation. The vividness of the presence can range from a vague feeling of being watched to a clearly perceived, seemingly flesh-and-blood entity."

McAndrew added that people were most likely to report experiencing supernatural phenomena in "threatening or ambiguous environments"—like, for example, living with the threat of a global virus—and that "sensed presences usually appear in environments with little variation in physical and social stimulation." Like, for example, when people are under extended stay-at-home orders.

With the collective trauma that the world has experienced during the pandemic, it could very well be that we are at the precipice of another large movement in interest in the supernatural. We are certainly well-equipped to discover the paranormal, with our increasingly connected world, our ever-improving technologies and our ability to share resources and information. ▪

Some people theorize the murderer hid in the attic of the house during the day before his midnight massacre.

VILLISCA, IOWA

THE AX MURDER HOUSE

The infamous location of eight gruesome murders has powerful paranormal activity that continues to lash out at investigators even today

THE BANNER HEADLINE ON THE FRONT PAGE OF *THE VILLISCA REVIEW* on June 13, 1912, informed the tiny Iowa community of the unspeakable crime that had taken place while the town had slumbered: "8 PEOPLE MURDERED IN THEIR BEDS IN VILLISCA." Somehow, an unknown assailant had gained access to the modest home belonging to Josiah and Sarah Moore and their four children, ages 5 to 11, the same night that two of their friends, Lena and Ina Stillinger, ages 11 and 8, were sleeping over. The man had drawn the shades, covered the mirrors with cloth and killed all of them with an ax belonging to Moore, before locking the door behind him and vanishing into the night.

In the months and years that followed, the case gripped the town's imagination. Various suspects were arrested and tried, but there was never conclusive evidence linking one definite perpetrator to the killings. Now, more than a century on, the murders remain a fixture in the imagination of true-crime aficionados and paranormal sleuths alike, both of whom are drawn to the house on Second Street where the unthinkably brutal acts of violence occurred.

When Amy and Adam visited the site, however, it was not for their usual sort of investigation. Rather, they went to Iowa to come to the aid of a friend in need—a mission that, in turn, brought them into contact with another wounded soul. Both men had experienced great personal suffering after encountering an entity on the premises, and it was only by returning to the Villisca Ax Murder House that they found healing and peace.

Amy and Adam tried several ways of communicating with the dangerous ghost of the Ax Murder House after an amateur investigator injured himself during his own dealings with the spirit.

AMY BRUNI: There was an investigator who was convinced that after he investigated there, his life was cursed. He had people near him who passed away or almost died. His name was John [Worley]. And he got an EVP [electronic voice phenomenon] there that said, "Just kill John Worley." He was terrified. That was new for us. We were like, "Okay, how do we fix this?"

ADAM BERRY: We had to test [his] theory. We had to get information, [so we began with the hypothesis that] well, maybe it is the house. John would not go in there, even when we were there with him. So, we would investigate [and ask], "Well, maybe there is somebody here that doesn't like John. What's the deal?"

We contacted another paranormal investigator, Robert Laursen Jr., who had an experience there where he thought the house tried to kill him. This investigator was on a private investigation with his parents—it was a gift for him for his birthday. He was in the downstairs room where the two friends were murdered. He was lying on the bed, and he did something that we don't normally do. It's called "provoking," so that means you're going to act aggressively toward whatever entity is in front of you to get a reaction. You're going to be mean. You're going to do whatever you can do to get a visceral reaction from the spirit. But he took it a step further.

AMY BRUNI: He had staged the house exactly as it had been found the morning of the murder. He covered all the mirrors with cloth, because the murderer for some reason found clothes and curtains and things and covered every mirror in the house with cloth. He had a bloody bowl of water in the kitchen. He had a slab of bacon, which for some reason, the killer had brought. But [Robert] didn't have an ax; he just

had a knife. So, that's what he had in his hand as he provoked, this knife.

ADAM BERRY: He lay down on the bed [holding] a knife. He said the only thing he remembers was he looked to his left, and this giant ball of light, this orb, came out of the closet toward him. The next thing he remembers was his father standing over him, pulling the knife out of his shoulder. He stabbed himself—with his nondominant hand, mind you. And he does not remember it.

AMY BRUNI: He was medevacked to the hospital. He coded due to blood loss and was revived.

ADAM BERRY: We met with him because when this came out publicly, everyone just thought he was crazy or he did it on purpose—it was a stunt, right? We met with him and got the story from him. There was nothing about him that would lead us to believe that he was lying to us. He genuinely had no idea what happened [before], and he still doesn't.

We got him to go back into that house. I think he wanted to make amends. He was afraid of that house. He wanted to confront whatever it was because he didn't understand what had happened to him. He lay down on the bed the same way he did [before]. He put his hand in a fist on his chest, and then he just started sobbing. He had this moment of release from whatever happened to him. When John Worley saw that, [it] helped him. You just have to face your fears sometimes.

AMY BRUNI: So [when] this [stabbing incident] happened, [Robert] had a camera set up—of course, this happens right out of frame. While he was in the hospital, his parents listened to the recorder, and they were so horrified by what they heard that they destroyed it. They don't ever want to revisit whatever happened in there. They won't talk about it. They didn't want him to talk to us. . . .

One of the main suspects in the murders was this man named Reverend Kelly. Five years later, he confessed and was tried for the crime, but he was acquitted based on insanity. He said that he had insomnia the night of the murders and walked by a nearby church and then went into this weird trance. He heard this voice tell him to "go further." When he got to the house, he heard the voice say, "Go on, follow the shadow and slay utterly." [Those] were the words that he heard "slay utterly." He found an ax—I guess the dad's ax—and went inside and killed the whole family. But it just sounded to me like such a similar situation to what happened to Robert. He went into this weird trance and then did something really awful. I can't confidently say that [house] is a safe place to investigate.

ADAM BERRY: I mean, we've never stopped investigating cases that stick with us. [We were] listening to this EVP that John Worley got, which, to us, sounds like "Just kill John Worley." Then Amy was doing some research while we were at the airport . . .

AMY BRUNI: One of the main suspects, William Blackie Mansfield, used the alias George

The killer washed up in the kitchen (above) and left a bowl of bloody water behind. He also covered the mirrors in the house with cloth (opposite bottom).

Worley to travel. Two years [after the Iowa murders], he killed his wife, his infant child, father-in-law and mother-in-law in Blue Island, Illinois, in their house with an ax and covered up all of the mirrors—literally the MO of the [Iowa] killer. He supposedly was someone who had traveled by train and maybe had committed a string of murders, ax murders. There are books written about this. [So] we listened to the EVP again, and it [might have said] "Just kill George Worley." Not John Worley.

ADAM BERRY: There was a theory that this guy who committed the murders sat in the attic all day, just waiting for the [family] to go to sleep. Other investigators who'd investigated the place [were] saying [the house] plays off of your fear. We tried an experiment where I sat with my back to the entrance of the attic—I hate having my back to open spaces. I was completely alone. We had a camera on a tripod filming me. Amy was listening to my audio in the building next door to make sure everything was okay because we didn't know what was going to happen. We were doing an EVP session asking, "Who are you? What did you do?" And it says right back to me, "I killed them." It was freaky. This person said, "I killed them. I killed them." Who that was, it didn't say, but that's why we feel like if there is anybody there, it's the murderer himself.

AMY BRUNI: There's also that idea that a space becomes infused with the energy put into it. The only energy that house sees is people walking into it day in and day out, talking about how six children and their parents were murdered in this house with an ax. That's it. Nobody's ever going to be in that house living a normal life ever again. It will just always be the "ax murder house." ■

With its long history of serving locals and travelers alike, it's possible that a couple of guests have never left this inn.

EAGLE BAY, NEW YORK

THE TOBOGGAN INN

Two spirit entities, two very different encounters

TUCKED AWAY IN A TINY HAMLET IN THE ADIRONDACK MOUNTAINS, the restaurant now operating as the Toboggan Inn has served hungry patrons since it was built in 1940. But when new owners Michael and Victoria Beck took over the historic business, they were surprised to find not one but two spirits inhabiting the property. The basement was home to an entity that seemed especially fond of the Becks—not only did it inhabit their newly acquired eatery, it also traveled home with them to their personal residence. "But that spirit was the least of our concerns," explains Amy.

Amy and Adam had to devote far more time and attention to managing the aggressive, masculine presence that dwelled upstairs, which seemed determined to harass and intimidate Victoria Beck and any other woman unlucky enough to happen onto its path. It took an especially effective spirit box (see page 58) session to get to the root of the haunting and help quell the disruptive supernatural behavior.

ADAM BERRY: Mike and Vicky Beck contacted us. They said that whatever was happening on the second floor, which was an unfinished apartment section of the property, was getting out of hand. We were basically begged to come because they wanted to make sure everyone was safe.

AMY BRUNI: There was a lot they caught on their security system. There were things flying, things moving, there was a lot of activity [directed] toward Vicky in particular. It seemed like the spirit upstairs especially did not like women and acted out toward her a lot. She was in tears. She told us, "I'm terrified up here." You'd go in the restaurant area, and it's all put together and nice and clean. You go upstairs, and there are walls knocked down. No one went up there for months because people kept getting attacked.

ADAM BERRY: [The second entity] was in the basement and seemed female in spirit. The family had said, "Whatever is here in this space follows us to the house." So, Amy came up with this brilliant idea. Amy and I were about to head over to their actual house that they live in. While in the basement, Amy said [to the entity], "We need to figure out if you're moving and going to the house. If you are, when we get over there, can you please tell us this secret word? Tell us the word 'apple.' " Sure enough, Amy and I and the Becks go over to their house, we're sitting on the couch, and Amy asks, "Can you tell me the secret word?" When we played back the recorder, the spirit says, "Apple."

AMY BRUNI: We were doing that to see if they actually had a spirit following them, because it's very rare. Some people just attract paranormal activity. Ghosts feel comfortable making themselves known to them. In this case, this spirit had followed them from an apartment they were in before to the house they had bought. We wanted to make sure that that was a safe spirit. Once we determined that [it was], we moved on to the one that was more violent. . . . When we

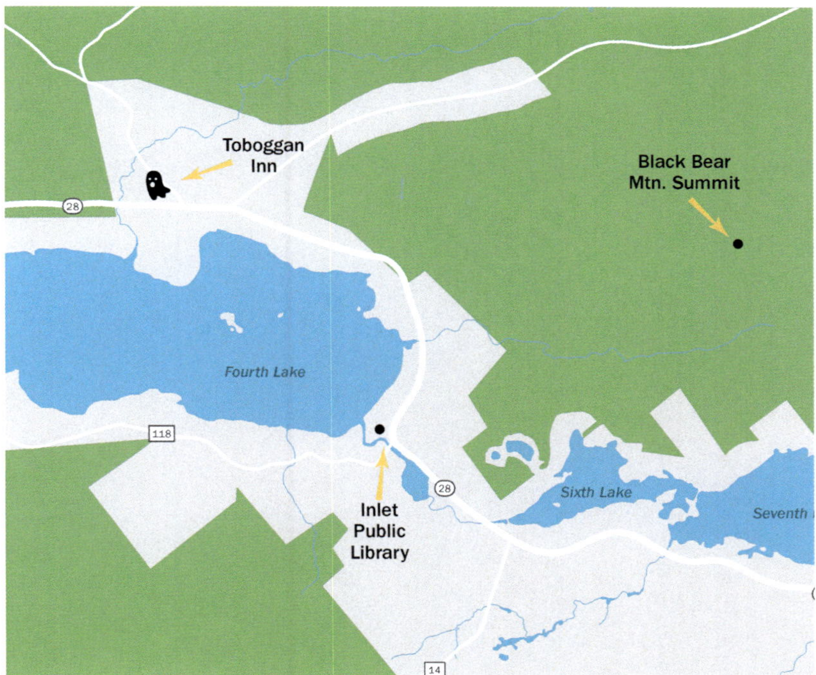

Things would move on their own in abandoned rooms (opposite). The spirit upstairs was particularly aggressive with women (above).

investigated this spirit, we realized it didn't like women. I was in the bathroom by myself, and Adam was in the other room with Chip [Coffey, a psychic medium], and I got this EVP in the recorder that I'm holding that says, "I'd love to be talking into this right now." It was so creepy.

ADAM BERRY: When you watch that video, you just see Amy sitting in the corner. You could feel that that dude was in that space with [her]. And for it to be that close in such an alarming way, it showed us what kind of character he was. His respect for women—there was none.

AMY BRUNI: We found out later—we did a pretty extensive spirit box session with him—and his mom apparently had left him when he was little. This male spirit harbored all this anger toward women. We always talk about being ghost therapists, but in that case, we really were.

ADAM BERRY: When we're doing the spirit box experiment, sometimes visuals pop into your head. You're trying to psychically connect with whatever's in that space. There came a point when I was sitting there . . . I got this extremely strong visual from a child's point of view—maybe a two year old, three year old's point of view—sitting on the ground, and the mother, the bottom half of her skirt, walking away from this kid and around the corner. It was so powerful and so vivid.

AMY BRUNI: I think Vicky Beck, once she knew what was going on, it put her more in control. She knew how to talk to this person.

ADAM BERRY: It's about [helping them get to a place where they're] taking back the space on their own. They're living. They have more power than the dead. They should use it.

Abandoned homes often seem creepy, but how do you find out if they're haunted?

THE GHOSTS NEXT DOOR

Every neighborhood—from the rural and remote to ones in the biggest cities—has its share of strange history and paranormal activity.

By Julie Tremaine

SO YOU'VE DECIDED TO start looking for ghosts. This is the beginning of a fascinating adventure, but fair warning: the deeper you research the paranormal, the more questions you will have. You might even start to second-guess things that you thought were absolute truths in your life.

The upside to studying the paranormal is that the field as we know it today is new enough that, if you have a unique perspective, you can make a valuable contribution to our collective understanding. Every leading expert in the field, including Amy Bruni and Adam Berry, started out as someone who spent their free time pursuing their interest in the paranormal and made a hobby of learning more about the things we can't explain. With years of study and work, these pursuits became careers. Both Amy and Adam started out as curious kids who were interested in the supernatural. They began exploring the world of ghost hunting on their own before gaining a reputation in the paranormal community. If you're passionate enough, you can make your mark.

IN YOUR BACKPACK

When you think of what you need to start searching for ghosts, your mind probably goes immediately to gear. What you need more than anything, though, is knowledge about your chosen site. Too many amateurs dive directly into investigating without doing their homework first. Read far and wide; take in everything you can get your hands on about the paranormal—not just about ghosts, but about UFOs and cryptids like Bigfoot, anything that piques your interest. The more you know about the world of weirdness, the more depth and unique value your perspective will hold.

A little bit of equipment can be helpful on a paranormal investigation—though it's not strictly necessary. While professional hunters may use many different pieces of technology, the equipment they use is secondary to the best asset they have: themselves. What do you see, hear, or smell in a given space? What is your sixth sense telling you? Are the hairs sticking up on the back of your arm? What does the energy of a room feel like? That information will inform you what to do next.

The one piece of equipment that you might want to invest in is a digital audio recorder—which is a device that is typically built into today's smartphones. The most common evidence that investigators capture is *electronic voice phenomena* (EVPs), which are recordings of spirits saying things that the human ear might not hear but that a recorder will pick up. Your phone works perfectly well for this, and as a bonus, it also has a flashlight to help when navigating those dark spaces.

The expensive equipment is definitely enticing, but you don't need it, especially when you're just starting out. While a structured light sensor (SLS) camera is fun to use, you don't *need* a piece of machinery that utilizes the motion detection technology (the kind that video game designers use) to track the location of entities in a space. You don't have to know where a spirit is in a room to be able to speak to it. You don't have to have K-II EMF meters that measure the electromagnetic frequencies in a space, but they can be helpful in detecting electrical interference that can cause hallucinations. When you're just getting started, all this technology can be more of

A local graveyard is a good place to investigate (opposite). If you're going into a building, make sure you have permission (this page).

a distraction than a help, and you might be too focused on the camera screen and miss what's happening in front of you. In the beginning, keep it simple.

WHERE GHOSTS APPEAR . . . AND WHY

There are endless theories about how and why certain places are haunted. It's impossible to know definitively which are correct—in part because ghosts are all individuals, just like people (after all, they were living people once), and they all behave differently. Some spirits will return to familiar places, like the homes where they lived as adults or where they grew up. Others will stay behind at or near the place they died, or at a place where a traumatic event occurred. Some will seek out something familiar, like a building of the time period when they were alive. Still more will seek out spots where they spent happy moments—which could be an explanation for why so many hotels are haunted.

There's also a school of thought that places aren't haunted, people are. It could be that spirits stay behind in family homes because they want to stay close to their loved ones. They could seek out people who are more receptive to seeing them, or who are more able to. In fact, the kind of person you bring with you to investigate could affect the outcome of your search. A staunch skeptic putting out negative energy can easily keep spirits away, whereas someone putting out welcoming energy can help attract them.

Another theory is that ghosts are attracted to particular energies, especially unsettled energy, like the kind generated during long periods of isolation. "For those whose experience of self-isolation involves what they believe to be a ghost," Molly Fitzpatrick wrote for the *New York Times* in May 2020, "their days are punctuated . . . by disembodied voices, shadowy figures, misbehaving electronics, invisible cats cozying up on couches, caresses from hands that aren't there and even, in some cases—to borrow the technical parlance of *Ghostbusters* —free-floating, full-torso vaporous apparitions."

Ghosts can be anywhere, at any time, for any reason. They can be found just as easily in the daytime as at night. So it stands to reason that

FREQUENTLY ASKED QUESTIONS

Top Five Signs a House Is Haunted

1. Do a gut check. Is your intuition going off? Are your spidey senses tingling? That's the first sign you might not be alone in a place. You don't have to be a psychic to sense that something is going on in a given space.

2. Are your pets behaving strangely? Owners of homes with paranormal activity often report that their dog will sit facing a corner and bark, or pay particular attention to one specific area of a house. That could be a sign there's something going on there.

3. You're hearing (or even smelling!) strange things. Slamming doors can easily be debunked if windows are open or there's a draft—but if you're hearing odd knocks, noises from other rooms or unusual voices, you might want to do some investigating.

4. Objects are moving on their own. A cabinet not properly installed could absolutely swing open on its own, but if things on shelves are shifting when no one is touching them, you might be dealing with a spirit.

5. You're having issues with electronics. Always change the batteries in the remote before you assume a ghost broke your television, but keep in mind that malfunctioning electronics are very common in energetically charged places.

Have you ever sensed a paranormal presence while in the woods?

if you're trying to make contact with one, you'll be able to find one pretty easily. In fact, there could be spirits in your house with you right now.

START THE INVESTIGATION NEAR HOME

If you're brave enough, investigating near your place of habitation is a great place to start, especially if you live in an older neighborhood or you've ever felt like you've sensed a presence in your home. That said, you want to make sure you can still fall sleep at night, so it's best not to rile up too much supernatural energy in your actual house. Your backyard or public spaces near your house that have some historical significance work perfectly. Do you live near an old park, or a graveyard? Those are excellent places to start your search.

Before you grab that flashlight and go on a hike, you'll want to make a pit stop at a local library or historical society. By doing research before you go on your search, you'll be arming yourself with as much knowledge as possible about a place. You won't just know who you might be looking for, you'll have background knowledge that will allow you to ask more specific questions and likely get much better results.

Libraries will have ownership records of homes, so you can find out who might have lived in a place before the current owners. They'll also have archives of old newspapers where you can search for any mysterious or particularly noteworthy deaths—unusual accidents, murders, disappearances.

Historical societies are your best resource for local legends and lore. The people who devote their time to knowing the minutiae about your town's history can help tell you where you should start your search. They will often have resources on hand that can help, like family histories and property deeds. They can also usually point you to people who have more information on specific locals, so you can ask deeper questions about a place's history.

TALKING TO GHOSTS

The thing to remember when making contact with spirits is that ghosts were once people. They aren't characters in horror movies conjured from the ether to terrify you. They should not be considered as a source of entertainment. We don't truly know why ghosts exist on the same plane as the living, but it seems likely that there's a reason: they want to be here, they don't know where else to go, or they need help with something.

While it can be fun and thrilling to seek out spirits, Amy and Adam suggest investigating with empathy. The more you talk

FREQUENTLY ASKED QUESTIONS

Phtographing Ghosts

It may sound counterintuitive, but ghost photos are some of the biggest points of contention for paranormal investigators. While it's technically possible to capture an entity on camera, it's extremely unlikely. Just look at how many times Amy and Adam have seen things appear on *Kindred Spirits* that the professional camera crew hasn't been able to capture. Even when they are able to capture video footage, it's almost always a blurry shape—not a clearly defined outline of a person.

Given how hard it is to capture a spirit in a photograph, even if you think you've got a picture of something that's definitely a ghost, it's probably not. Bugs or spiderwebs across a lens can create an eerie effect in a photograph, as can dust in the air or smudges. And that shadow person you swear wasn't there in the shot of your friends? It's probably just a weird shadow or a person you didn't notice when you took the photo.

to ghosts like they're people too, the better results you'll get—but you might find yourself in a situation where the entities you encounter need your help in some way. That's why it's so important to do research. If a ghost doesn't know why it's in a place, it might need your help to figure out what happened and give them the information they've been lacking.

THE KINDS OF GHOSTS YOU MIGHT FIND

There are as many ways spirits can present themselves as there are unique people in the world—more, actually, if you consider how many people have lived and died already. But in general, they fall into a few broad categories.

A spirit or apparition is an energetic being who, usually, has chosen to stay behind for a reason. (Some people believe spirits can come in and out of this plane, so an apparition may have just chosen to appear at a particular moment in time.) Their reason could be anything from attachment to a home, object or person, to unfinished business. Spirits engaged in this kind of presence are generally called active hauntings.

What you may see or hear in an active haunting can vary widely. A ghost can appear as a full- or partial-body apparition, but more often they will appear as a hazy shape or energy disruption in the atmosphere. Sometimes they appear as orbs of light, and sometimes they only make their presence known by knocking, making noise, or moving objects.

When something traumatic happens in a space, it can leave an energetic imprint in that space. Think of a room where you've felt tension or fear, like a hospital room, and how those feelings seem to linger afterward. Sometimes, if the event is big enough, a residual haunting can occur, which is usually defined as an energetic imprint that happens over and over. If the same action repeats itself, but you aren't able to communicate with a spirit, it could be a residual haunting.

Rarely, you could encounter something that isn't just a benign spirit, such as a poltergeist. The term *poltergeist* comes from the German for "noisy spirits," and this type of entity is a known troublemaker. Poltergeists have been known to make loud noises, repeatedly knock things over, move furniture or shake beds. Poltergeists are most commonly associated with teenage girls and are often reported in homes where teenage girls live.

While people are quick to assume that a presence in a space is "evil" or "demonic," those are the absolute rarest of cases, and the ones where you should not investigate on your own. In these very rare cases, the activity is not limited to scratches or scary-sounding noises. Instead, it's severe activity like furniture being smashed by unseen forces, or a person speaking in a

Libraries and historical societies (bottom) are good places to start investigating locations you think might be haunted (top).

language they don't know. If you are experiencing something that severe, consult an experienced paranormal investigator—or even a religious leader—for help.

STAYING SAFE

Paranormal investigation is best done with someone you trust. There are reasons the researchers on reality ghost hunting shows always work in pairs: not just because it's much more productive to work in teams, but also because you could encounter animals or living people who could be dangerous to you. (And remember: While ghosts could possibly scratch or touch you, they're not generally trying to hurt you. They're just trying to communicate.)

If you want to investigate private or restricted property, you always have to seek permission when necessary and abide by the property's rules. If a cemetery closes at dusk and you'd be trespassing if you went in the middle of the night, then investigate during the day. It may feel spookier to investigate at night, but ghosts exist all the time, not just after sundown. They aren't more likely to talk to you in the dark. There's no quicker way to dampen your chances of success than to get kicked out of a place by security, or worse, arrested.

If you can establish a good relationship with a local historic house museum or other point of interest that you think might be haunted, and you can prove to the powers that be at that place that you are well-intentioned and respectful, they might grant you after-hours access. It all comes down to doing the homework to find out which places are worth exploring, and then contacting those places in ways that show the owners or managers that you can be trusted. After that, the place is yours . . . at least for a night. ■

You can visit the cells of the prison—if you're not claustrophobic.

ST. AUGUSTINE, FLORIDA

OLD ST. JOHNS COUNTY JAIL

Beautiful on the outside, cruel within—this prison has a storied past that's trying to make itself known

BY THE END OF THE 19TH CENTURY, IN ST. AUGUSTINE, FLORIDA, hotelier Henry Flagler had amassed a number of high-end, luxury properties that were becoming favored destinations among America's wealthiest travelers. But Flagler was concerned that the local jail was simply too close for comfort to one of his chic hot spots—so, he paid to have it demolished and had a new one built in its current location in the Romanesque revival style. The exterior of the newly constructed facility was as fetching as the other buildings in Flagler's real estate portfolio, but the façade concealed unspeakable horrors.

Until the jail was decommissioned in 1953, dozens of inmates were kept imprisoned in deplorable conditions—for a while without access to running water or basic sanitation. Women worked in the kitchen, while men were leased out to local farmers as field hands, shackled together at the ankles. Malnutrition and disease were commonplace; some prisoners were beaten and tortured. Eight inmates were hanged at the site. Among them were two men, James Kirby and Robert Lee, who were put to death in 1901 for the murder of a local man, despite Kirby's insistence that he alone committed the act. Lee's own repeated protestations of innocence fell on deaf ears.

These days, the Old Jail is open to the public for tours that show men laboring in chain gangs and some of the other hardships prisoners endured there. Statues stand in for the tortured prisoners, but many of the unfortunate souls who were condemned to suffer within the jail's walls are believed to linger on the premises. Amy and Adam, along with psychic medium Chip Coffey, encountered an array of spirits during their investigation of the premises—including the spectral presence of Lee himself.

AMY BRUNI: When we investigated at that jail, I feel like it was just the tip of the iceberg. While we were there, it seemed like there were so many ghosts that wanted to make themselves known. We saw shadow figures, we heard footsteps. The manager had been pushed at one point.

ADAM BERRY: We were contacted because they had had activity in the past, [and] they wanted to make sure that the patrons would be safe. People go there to learn about this jail, but what people don't realize is the way that people were kept in that jail in the early part of the century . . . was not the best.

AMY BRUNI: Adam and I kept commenting on how you're in this jail that's a huge tourist attraction, and you're sitting there and you're watching kids walking by eating ice cream. People [are] laughing and [saying], "Oh, this is so creepy." But I don't think they fully understand what went on there.

ADAM BERRY: Amy saw a shadow crawl across the floor. Then I saw it go up the wall. . . . We started doing EVP work, and a voice came through and said, "I'm not a murderer." We knew it sounded male, but that could've been any one

The Old Jail is now a museum (above) that gives a glimpse of what prison life was like for the jailers and the jailed (opposite).

of the people that had been there in the past. It could have been lying to us. [So] we had to dig through the history of that location and really pinpoint who this person was. We uncovered newspaper articles that talked about a specific incident, these two men who were accused of murder. On the day that they were put to death, one of them confessed that the other one had nothing to do with the murder itself. The falsely accused man, Robert Lee, said, "The truth will come out, if not in this life, the next."

AMY BRUNI: We say this a lot when we go into asylums or prisons—don't go in with preconceived notions. Don't go in with this idea that you're only going to encounter bad people, because a lot of the people that ended up in those old jails, they were specifically brought there to work on the chain gang. They were arrested for the sole purpose of serving that sheriff. I mean, these men were forced to catch rats and eat them and things. [That's] yet another reason why those spirits would be at such unrest.

ADAM BERRY: They were forced to build their own gallows, too. They were forced to build the thing that was going to ultimately put them to death. . . . We started using [Robert Lee's] name, talking out loud to see if it was him, and we were getting more and more evidence. We were able to eventually talk [with Lee directly]. Amy put herself in the jail with some whiskey to coax him out.

AMY BRUNI: We stressed to the manager of the jail to tell Lee's story a lot. It was important for them to get this story out there accurately, to maybe make it a regular part of their tours, so people learned the correct history behind it. ■

Amy and Adam brought sophisticated gear to help them with this investigation.

OGDENSBURG, NEW JERSEY

STERLING HILL MINE

A lot of things can go wrong in a mine, and some accidents echo across time, deep down in the earth

"FEARLESS" SEEMS LIKE IT MIGHT BE A FITTING DESCRIPTION FOR someone who investigates hauntings for a living, but both Amy and Adam insist there have been plenty of times in their careers when they have found themselves at the very least uncomfortable, if not outright terrified. For the claustrophobic Amy, visiting the Sterling Hill Mine in northwestern New Jersey forced her to face several of her worst fears, along with her least favorite paranormal manifestation.

"Being underground is hard for me; I don't like it at all," Amy says. "Elevators I have a big problem with. I don't like the idea of earth above me. I feel like it could cave in at any moment. I grew up in northern California where there are lots of mines, and so I know a lot about miners and what they had to endure working underground. . . . It's so uncomfortable. I could not shake that the whole time we were investigating there. On top of that, hearing creepy, growling disembodied voices in the darkness didn't help."

One of those voices seemed to belong to the spirit of a man named Frank Carroll who once worked as a cage operator at the mine, which operated from 1897–1986 extracting deposits of iron and zinc ore. In 1958, Carroll was ferrying miners to and from the surface. After he exited the conveyance, it plummeted 500 feet, slamming into the ground, tragically killing miners Ralph Romyns and Lou Davenport. While Carroll was unharmed, Amy notes that Carroll's spirit has "remained in the mine, because he felt so guilty about the accident that resulted in those deaths." When she and Adam explored the site, they encountered Carroll's unhappy spirit—who seemed unwilling or unable to leave the location behind.

ADAM BERRY: Miners were lost in the mine and never came back. Back in the day, they had lamps that were oil-[fueled] lanterns—the thing that you need to survive in a mine when you're thousands of feet under the ground is light. And if their light went out, or if it broke, they would not find their way out of the mine. They would die in that environment. So, for us, going in there, we didn't know what to expect. As we're walking around inside of the space, reaching out to anyone that might be there, we were encountering noises and sounds as if the mine was in operation. I remember we were investigating with a person that worked in the mine because we needed to confirm what these sounds were. We were all standing by the elevator entrance to go down into the mine, and we heard this rumble. We were like, "What is that sound?" And he says, "It sounds like an ore car." But that would be impossible because there's nobody working this mine, clearly.

AMY BRUNI: Also, it was flooded underneath us. . . . We were zeroing in on this accident that happened that we thought might be fueling the haunting. We started getting closer and closer to where it happened. We were standing there, and all of a sudden, all of the power goes off in the mine. And it didn't just go off—it was doing this weird cycling thing where the lights were dimming and then coming back on. It was so wild. The poor kid who was our security guy was just freaking out. He was like, "I've never seen this happen before." The timing was really odd. [It happened] as soon as we started digging into this accident where these two men perished because they suspect the person who was operating the elevator stepped off for a second and you're never supposed to do that.

This shot was taken while the power was on (opposite). Once it went off, Amy, Adam and their crew were plunged into darkness. Products made with fluorescent minerals that came from the mine (above).

ADAM BERRY: We were in the middle of this mine shaft. It's rigged with lights now because it's a museum of sorts. But we're standing there, and we are reaching out to this guy, saying, "We're here for a purpose. The purpose is those that take care of this place for you want to make sure that you're okay, and we have the tools to do that. So, hear us out for the time being." And it seemed to work. We were getting responses from this gentleman. And then all the lights went out inside of this mine. What's the one thing that miners cannot be without? It's light. So, [this entity] literally took our sight away. They were like, "You're done. You're not going to be doing this anymore. You're not going to be talking." We knew at that point we needed to get out of there. We're on the right track, but whatever guilt that man is feeling—we felt like he felt guilty, he had remorse about it—it's enough. [We decided], let's let him process what's going on.

AMY BRUNI: It felt like it was one of those self-imposed sentence situations. Even though he went on to live out his life—he did not die in the accident—he kept coming back. It was this thing that haunted him in life, and so he kept going back to that spot, revisiting what happened as a spirit. You could tell there was guilt there—his spirit was there because of that accident.

ADAM BERRY: It's almost like [he was saying], "I don't want to be okay, so stop doing what you're doing." We weren't justifying what he did, but we were shining light on it and telling him, "Whatever happened, it happened, and you don't have to be in this space. You don't necessarily have to be down in this mine by yourself." In his own time, maybe he'll feel like leaving when he thinks he's done his sentence. ▪

Producing pig iron at the furnaces was dangerous—and sometimes deadly—work.

BIRMINGHAM, ALABAMA

SLOSS FURNACES

Long hours, a cruel foreman and dangerous working conditions were business as usual at this iron processing plant

IN 1881, WEALTHY SOUTHERN MERCHANT JAMES WITHERS SLOSS broke ground on a new 50-acre facility on the outskirts of Birmingham, Alabama, that was designed to wisely exploit the region's abundant deposits of iron ore and coal. When Sloss Furnaces opened for business a year later, men desperate for work immediately came calling. But the employees were subjected to unbelievably dangerous and grueling conditions as they labored to produce vast quantities of pig iron. Hours were long, and accidents were commonplace. According to the stories, the tenure of one graveyard shift supervisor, James "Slag" Wormwood, proved especially deadly—at least 47 workers lost their lives on his watch, with another six blinded and many others suffering grave injuries. Eventually, the furnaces claimed Wormwood himself; in 1906, he fell into a pool of molten ore and was killed instantly.

These days, Sloss Furnaces has become a National Historic Landmark site, hosting concerts, festivals and conferences, along with workshops and exhibitions of metal art, yet echoes of the past remain. Amy and Adam, who visited the site with musician, actor and paranormal enthusiast Meat Loaf, felt Wormwood's presence. He seemed determined to continue to menace anyone unlucky enough to encounter him.

AMY BRUNI: Sloss Furnaces was a big iron-producing blast furnace, and it was in operation from 1882 to 1970. It saw a lot of atrocious industrial accidents. There were stories of one guy where some steam tunnel exploded, and literally, his skin just melted off—just the most horrible, horrible ways for people to die. That gave way to a lot of its haunted reputation. Adam and I were at one point using the laser grid, and we definitely saw this shadow. We were actually investigating with Meat Loaf—he's come out with us a few times. We call him Meat, by the way, which is ironic because he's a vegetarian. So, we were investigating in this tunnel, and we just watched this shadow figure. It kept walking out. It would look at us and then hide. It started walking toward us at one point.

ADAM BERRY: He was about my height. We were using the laser grid, which basically is a device that shines dots of lasers down a dark hallway, and sometimes an entity will step into the lasers [and] blocks out dots. It felt like that person was an overseer of sorts, as if he was in charge of the space. I got the feeling he did not like us being in that space. [He gave off a feeling of] "We have work to do, there are things we're doing. There

Amy and Adam felt like they were being followed by a shadow figure, which may have been the spirit of the supervisor who died there.

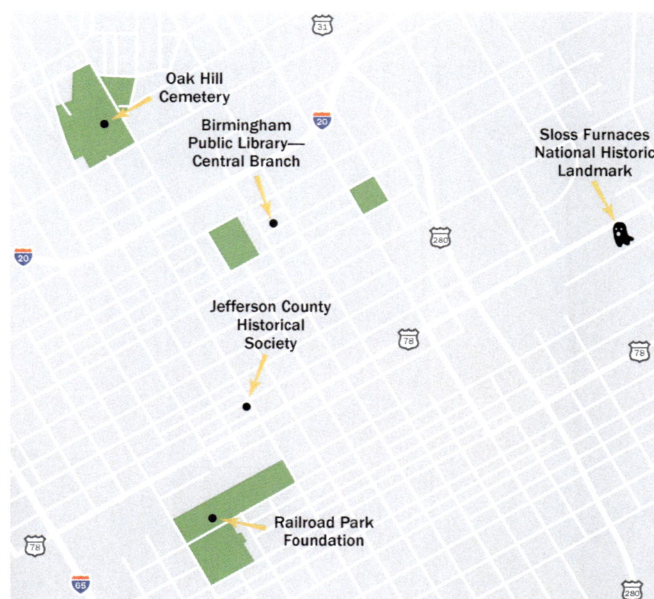

isn't time for this kind of thing." That's the reputation that spirit has gotten, and I did get the sense that we were bugging him and wasting his time.

AMY BRUNI: I remember walking by myself at one point and hearing footsteps behind me in the gravel. I was just trying to get from point A to point B, and I thought someone was playing a joke on me. I would turn around and there was no one there. . . . I have this theory that if I hum or whistle, nothing bad can happen, so I remember trying to get to where I was going, whistling and humming [with] these footsteps behind me the whole way. So strange.

ADAM BERRY: The way we investigate and the way we interact with whoever we're trying to reach out to—I don't know if it's our energy or the way we work together—we tend to gain their trust or get their attention. I believe it's the way that we do things and the way that we operate that facilitates that. You don't always walk into a haunted place and see a shadow figure. But if you play your cards right, and if you investigate with integrity—you are treating them like a person and you're being sympathetic—they tend to reach out a little bit more frequently.

AMY BRUNI: Yeah. I mean, there [was a lot of activity]. The local law enforcement would [allegedly] go into cahoots with the people who ran these places. They would use convict laborers. The sheriff would go out and start just arresting random people and then making them work on the chain gang. A lot of those guys died there. It's awful.

ADAM BERRY: A lot of energy, too, is left behind. It creates haunts. When you're there, you literally smell mothballs—that's a by-product of mining—[even though the mining operation has] been shut down for years and years. ▪

Some of the sixth installment in the Jason movies was filmed in the park.

MORGAN COUNTY, GEORGIA

CAMP RUTLEDGE

Inside the confines of Hard Labor Creek State Park, you'll find Camp Rutledge, which is thought to be one of the most haunted places in the state

WITNESSES HAVE DESCRIBED TWO DIFFERENT ENTITIES THAT RESIDE at Camp Rutledge. One is the spirit of a man who has been known to knock on cabin walls and slam doors. The other is thought to be the ghost of a child named Ethan, who disappeared from the camp in 1973. In the years since, he's been glimpsed behind trees, and he appears to have in his possession a red, rubber ball. (Amplifying the spooky factor? The 1986 slasher film *Friday the 13th Part VI: Jason Lives* was shot on location at the state park.)

As part of an investigation at the site, Adam decided to spend the night in one of the camp's cabins. Although he heard strange, unsettling sounds during his stay, the noises turned out to have an entirely natural explanation—they were made by a very active nest of bees. Adam and Amy agree: this is a good reminder that not every seemingly inexplicable occurrence is rooted in the paranormal.

ADAM BERRY: There was a kid named Ethan who drowned in one of the lakes there. [People] see this child. They find footprints of wet feet in the dining hall. Also, there's this specific cabin where somebody was sleeping in it, and they heard someone say, "You'll die here." They saw some shadow, and it said, "You'll die here"—which is unnerving if you're in a cabin in the middle of the woods.

AMY BRUNI: Probably if you've experienced it, I think it's unnerving for anyone [to hear a disembodied voice]. Your hackles go up because it's just wrong. It's like the first time I tried to go scuba diving, my body was like, "You're not supposed to breathe underwater." You're not supposed to hear a voice coming out of thin air where a mouth would be if someone were standing there, but no one is there. It's like this fight-or-flight moment where your instinct takes over, and it can be very triggering. It doesn't feel natural because almost every time you hear a disembodied voice, it's not like it floats out of a closet or something. Almost every time, it literally is right next to you where a mouth would be if someone were standing there. That's why it's so weird. You're like, "What the hell?"

ADAM BERRY: I went to that cabin and in the aim of making it as real as possible for any entity that might be there; I was going to go to sleep. I got the sleeping bag out. I put it on the bottom bunk, and I lay down on that bunk just to see if this thing would reach out and say anything. I did hear what sounded like scratching on the side of the cabin, which is also another thing that happens there. [It's] said this entity goes around and bangs on the cabin and scratches on it. Now, could it have been the same person that said, "You'll die here"? Maybe? But it did not say that I would die, thank God, because I didn't want to go out like

One of the spirits haunting the cabins is thought to be that of a child who drowned in the lake.

that. I was more afraid of the spiders to be perfectly honest.

AMY BRUNI: So that was one of my first cases, I was pregnant and very tired, and I was like, "Yeah, my pregnant ass is not sleeping in this wooden little cabin," so I got out. I do remember feeling bad. They were done for the season so [the cabins] were just dirty. But we figured out it was carpenter bees causing the scratching sounds. We were like, "This has to be the scratching," because they were massive. There were so many of them.

ADAM BERRY: Anything scratching on a cabin in the middle of the night is terrifying. If you can explain it away, that's great. But it's really interesting to think about being in the woods, being alone and what tricks your mind plays [on you]. Any sound outside—of sticks breaking or leaves rustling—you immediately think the worst, especially in an environment like that. I think it plays into all the spooky stories and folklore of that location. . . . The purpose of us being there is to have these experiences so we can either explain them away or continue to make contact with [any entities that might be in the space]. There could be something at this camp, but with all outdoor locations, it could be the spirit of a little boy who drowned in a lake, or it could be something of an earthly nature, like an elemental spirit that's being mischievous and started wreaking havoc on the campers.

AMY BRUNI: It's just as valuable to find a non-paranormal cause as a paranormal cause. As long as we find a cause, that's really our ultimate goal. When we realize there's really no explanation, that's when we start freaking out. ■

OUR HAUNTED AMERICA

This great land has its fair share of haunted locations, and many of them trace their paranormal origins back to dramatic moments in the nation's history.

By Julie Tremaine

Your next paranormal experience might be just down the highway.

YOU'VE DONE YOUR homework, you've researched paranormal investigation techniques and you're prepared to scare yourself silly in the name of research and good fun. It's official: you're ready to hit the road. No matter where you are in America, or anywhere else in the world, the good news is you're never very far from a haunted location.

KNOW BEFORE YOU GO

Is there one notoriously spooky place you've always dreamed of exploring? While there's no time like the present to explore, with most locations, you won't have full access to the place without some homework. Start your trip by researching the places you're dreaming of visiting. Are they closed seasonally? Only open some days of the week? Sold out for the rest of the year?

Determine your supernatural plan of attack by gathering as much information as possible as well as strategies for how to investigate once you're there. You'll also want to decide whether you really want to sleep in haunted hotels—or just visit them. Whether you're truly investigating for ghosts or just visiting for fun, you'll make some new memories and learn new things about history as you go.

YOUR PERSONALIZED PARANORMAL TRIP

There are a lot of ways to approach exploring strange destinations. You could set out to visit one of the places listed here that's closer to where you live, or string together a few and make your own road trip itinerary. Online mapping tools are helpful for putting together routes: for example, Google Maps not only tells you the distance and driving time between places (including time

Salem, Massachusetts, has memorials, museums and annual events devoted to the witch trials.

zone changes), it allows you to drag and drop the order of your stops to more easily decide which places you want to go in which order, and even customize the roads you take to get there.

OLD HAUNTED SPOTS IN NEW ENGLAND

One of the great parts about New England, the six small states in the northeastern-most corner of the United States, is that there is a *lot* of history in a very concentrated space, which easily lets you hit multiple spots on one trip. Home to some of the oldest European colonies, New England has haunted history spanning more than 400 years.

If you're looking for a site with a dark history that has embraced its complicated past, there's no place better than the very spooky Salem, Massachusetts, site of the 17th-century Salem Witch Trials. Salem, founded by British colonists in 1626, was overtaken by mass hysteria surrounding witchcraft in 1692. More than 150 people were accused of witchcraft, and 19 people were executed for performing "the Devil's magic."

If you've only got a day or two to visit, make sure to see the Witch House museum, the former home of a judge involved in the trials, and Proctor's Ledge, where the convicted were hanged, which is now a memorial to them. Salem is especially popular around Halloween, but you can take walking "Witch City" tours of the city's spookiest locations at any time of year. When it's time to turn in, spend the night at the Hawthorne Hotel . . . if you dare.

Built in 1925 on land owned by one of the women executed for witchcraft, the Hawthorne Hotel is an ideal place to investigate for paranormal activity. People have reported seeing a woman outside

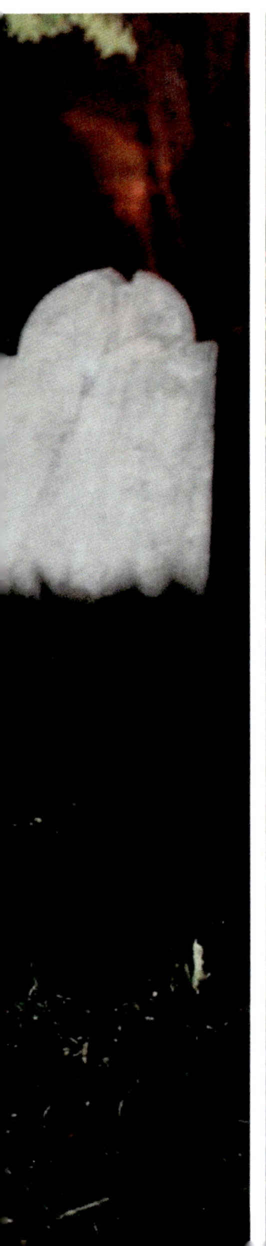

The Wren Building in Williamsburg, Virginia, has a long history of war and fire.

room 612 and unexplained activity in room 325.

Salem isn't the only place in New England where people were wrongfully accused of brushes with the supernatural. Mercy Brown, accused of being a vampire in 1892 when she passed away at 19 years old in Exeter, Rhode Island, was part of a family that that had many people die of a wasting disease we now know is tuberculosis.

Because tuberculosis wasn't understood at the time but was widespread through the region, supernatural explanations prevailed, leading to the New England Vampire Panic at the end of the 19th century. Because most of the Brown family was affected, superstition dictated that the deceased family should be exhumed. Mercy's mother and sister were decomposed, but Mercy's body was well-preserved and still had blood in her heart. Locals assumed she had to be the vampire killing her family members. Neighbors burned her heart and fed it to her younger brother to attempt to rescue him from the disease, to no avail. (Really, she died in winter, and her body was preserved because it was frozen.)

Mercy Brown was buried in Chestnut Hill Cemetery in Exeter, and her remains are there to this day, and the legend of New England's most famous "vampire" lives on.

Not all of New England's haunted history is scary, though. At the famously haunted Omni Mount Washington Resort in Bretton Woods, New Hampshire, many who work there say they've either seen or felt something unexplained, and there are countless stories of guests both living and dead coming into contact with each other. The most famous of those ghosts: that of owner Carolyn Stickney, whose husband built the hotel in 1902 and passed away the following year. Her second husband was a prince, making her Princess Carolyn for the later years of her life. Carolyn's personal quarters in room 314, now known as the Carolyn Stickney Suite, still has her original four-poster bed and is where she's commonly spotted by those who believe to have encountered her.

MID-ATLANTIC BATTLEFIELDS AND HISTORIC LANDMARKS

Historic battlefields are some of the most active paranormal spots you can visit—and because so many of them are National Historic Sites, they're well-preserved and easy to access.

Williamsburg, Virginia, is one of the most historically important locations in the country, where events spurring the Revolutionary War transpired. The beautifully preserved Colonial Williamsburg is a living history museum, and the area is absolutely full of reports of haunted encounters. One of the most active spots: the Wren. The Wren Building is part of William & Mary, one of the oldest universities in the country. It was used as a hospital during the American Revolution and the Civil War, and burned down three times. There's even a crypt in the basement.

If you're searching for the spirits of the Civil War, there's no better place to explore than Gettysburg, Pennsylvania. The site of the bloodiest battle of the Civil War, over 7,000 people lost their lives in the 1863 conflict at Gettysburg, and there are endless stories of ghost sightings there to this day. Adam Berry had his first true glimpse of the paranormal there, where he heard disembodied voices and what he thought were gunshots in a field at night. Any *Kindred Spirits* fan knows that's the experience that truly spurred his interest in ghosts. The town is full of ghost tours and places to investigate, but when you're done for the night, make camp at the Gettysburg Campground, where people have reported otherworldly sights and sounds.

Another important location in American military history is Fort McHenry in Baltimore, Maryland. The site of the War of 1812 battle where the flag flew that inspired Francis Scott Key to write "The Star-Spangled Banner," Fort McHenry is also allegedly one of the most haunted spots in the city. During the Civil War, Confederate sympathizers and soldiers were imprisoned there, and to this day people report hearing disembodied voices and footsteps, seeing lights come on for no reason, and smelling gunpowder in the air. Nearby, in Baltimore's Inner Harbor, the USS *Constellation* is a pre-Civil War ship which allows overnight stays, where people say they see apparitions walking the decks and peering through portholes.

THE SPOOKY SOUTHWEST

The untamed history of the Wild West is all around you in the desert states of the Southwest.

FREQUENTLY ASKED QUESTIONS

Gaining Access to Haunted Locations

There are a lot of ways to think about what constitutes a haunted location. Historic sites like battlefields and old cemeteries certainly have the possibility of being haunted, and those are open to the public and often free of charge.

Haunted hotels are another easy and fun place to start, and all you need to do is book a room. Many of the most haunted spots in hotels are public spaces like the lobby and the ballroom, or even just hallways—so you might not even need to stay overnight to experience them. Some hotels lean into their haunted histories, like the Omni Mount Washington Resort in New Hampshire's White Mountains or the *Queen Mary*, a former cruise ship that's now a permanently docked hotel in Long Beach, California. Both of those places allow you to stay overnight in their spookiest rooms for a higher room rate. (Ghosts, apparently, cost extra.)

If you're dreaming about doing an overnight investigation in a haunted mansion turned museum or an old asylum like Waverly Hills Sanatorium in Louisville, Kentucky, that's going to take a little bit more work. You'll need to reach out to the owners, introduce yourself, and ask special permission to be there—and getting a yes will likely take something of an established reputation or an affiliation with a reputable paranormal research group. A place that is difficult to gain access to is not one where you should begin your ghost hunting career in, however. If you only have one night in a space, you want to have mastery over your equipment and some established investigating techniques that you know work well for you before you go. The good news is that many difficult-to-access locations offer ghost tours or guided investigations, which are great ways to start relationships with the places you most want to explore.

From abandoned ghost towns to haunted locations that saw some of the most iconic moments in American history—the O.K. Corral, anyone?—there is so much of the supernatural to explore.

Sedona, Arizona, is a massive energy vortex believed to be a center of energy healing and otherworldly experiences. The places in the area where the energy is strongest—and communication should be easiest to facilitate because of that supercharged energy—are Airport Mesa, Cathedral Rock, Bell Rock and Boynton Canyon. Even if you aren't able to make contact with the other side, you'll likely benefit from the experience: visitors report feeling happier, lighter and more energized after going.

Another place full of 19th century legends and hauntings: Tombstone, Arizona. Stories of the paranormal are everywhere in this town, from the O.K. Corral where Wyatt Earp had his famous shootout to Big Nose Kate's Saloon, which dates back to 1880 and is still slinging beers on its original bar. It's easy to find a ghost tour that will take you to the most notoriously haunted spots, like the Birdcage Theatre, which has alternately been a theatre, saloon, brothel and gambling parlor, and where legend has it that 26 people died over the years it was open. In 1882, the *New York Times* called the Bird Cage the wickedest night spot between Basin Street and the Barbary Coast.

But if that has too many living people for you, check out New Mexico's abandoned ghost towns instead. The state has so many that New Mexico has an official ghost town map on its website (www.newmexico.org/places-to-visit/ghost-towns). Of particular note: Shakespeare, an abandoned mining town which offers ghost town tours that include the interiors of seven buildings, and Lincoln, which was the historical home of Billy the Kid and hosts an

FREQUENTLY ASKED QUESTIONS

Ghost Hunting Equipment

You don't truly *need* anything to investigate the paranormal other than your own senses and innate curiosity—and maybe a notebook and pen. But if you want to enhance your investigative techniques, you could use one or more of the gadgets below.

Handheld audio recorder: The one in your smartphone works perfectly well, but investing in a small handheld device that has better noise filtering or allows you to make timestamps on the file when there's something worth noting can save you some time and hassle when you're reviewing evidence later.

Flashlight: Necessary if you're in a dark location, but it's workable to use your smartphone flashlight, too.

KII-EMF Meter: This device measures electromagnetic frequency in a space. High EMF can cause visual and auditory hallucinations and other side effects that people sometimes attribute to ghosts, so more than anything, it's a helpful tool in debunking paranormal activity, not finding it.

Spirit Box: This machine scans electronic waves to pick up supernatural interference, and it's a tool that Amy and Adam use on almost every episode of *Kindred Spirits*. The downsides are that the responses happen in real time, so you can't play them back to listen again, and that it takes some real practice to differentiate what's a faint radio signal and what's paranormal.

SLS Camera: A structured light sensor camera can track an unseen entity's presence in a space by utilizing the same motion tracking that video game developers use. While it's really cool to see a ghost's location, this is an expensive tool that you definitely don't need to splurge on when you're just starting out.

Big Nose Kate's Saloon in Tombstone, Arizona, is still slinging suds, 140 years after the shootout at the O.K. Corral.

annual reenactment of "The Last Escape of Billy the Kid."

THE WEIRD HISTORY OF CALIFORNIA

Europeans first visited California 65 years before the establishment of the first settlement let alone the 13 original colonies on America's East Coast, and the Golden State has endless spooky stories to explore.

Growing up in the San Francisco Bay Area, Amy Bruni spent her childhood exploring haunted spots, from Fort Ross in Sonoma County that has a centuries-old Russian burying ground to the Phoenix Theatre, a concert venue in Petaluma that's so haunted that a song has been written about it. One of the most haunted spots: the USS *Hornet*, a retired World War II aircraft carrier turned museum docked in Alameda that's a known paranormal hotspot. The museum hosts regular History Mystery Tours and will even do ghost tours.

Californians have had many brushes with paranormal military history, including the heir of the Winchester Rifle fortune, who believed she was being pursued by ghosts of people who had died by her family's weapons. Sarah Winchester started renovating a house she bought there in 1886, and continued to build the house up to 160 rooms with 10,000 windows and 2,000 doors—and staircases leading to nowhere—until her death in 1922. Legend says that Winchester kept building onto the home because construction would confuse the ghosts of the people who had been killed by her family's weapons, and they would never find her. Now, the Winchester Mystery House hosts property tours and spooky ghost tours.

The Winchester Mystery House might be the most notorious paranormal destination in the state, but there are more famous ghosts to be found in Los Angeles, especially at its historic hotels like the Hollywood Roosevelt Hotel on Hollywood Boulevard, built in 1927, where the first Oscars ceremony was held. Marilyn Monroe lived in room 1200 for a time, and there are frequent reports of her ghost appearing inside the hotel to this day. The Chateau Marmont, built in 1929 on Sunset Boulevard, is where John Belushi died in 1982. His Bungalow 3 is rife with rumors of sightings of a "funny man."

THE GHOSTS OF THE MIDDLE STATES

One of the country's most legendarily scary hotels, a haunted prison and a town so full of spirits that it calls itself America's Halloween Town—what more could you want?

The most famous artistic representation of a haunted hotel—Stephen King's *The Shining*—was inspired by a stay at The Stanley Hotel in Estes Park, Colorado. The building has more than 100 years of haunted history, including legends of the ghosts of Mr. and Mrs. Stanley appearing to guests, disembodied laughter and objects

Fans gather at the Winchester House to support the 2018 release of the film with Helen Mirren about the storied mansion (this page). The Fairmont Banff Springs Hotel in Alberta, Canada, has a room allegedly so haunted, it's sealed from the public (opposite).

moving on their own. The Ultimate Stanley "Spirit" Experience will get you a room on the most active fourth floor and your own EMF meter, but there are also night tours of the spooky history open to everyone.

Another place to take hair-raising night tours: Missouri State Penitentiary in Jefferson City, Missouri, which hasn't had inmates since 2004—well, *living* inmates, anyway. A notoriously haunted spot with a huge amount of paranormal activity, Missouri State Penitentiary now offers history tours where you can see the gas chamber that executed more than 40 prisoners, or paranormal tours that highlight the spirits most often experienced in the historic space.

Going on a ghost tour is one thing, but if you want to dig deeper into an investigation, you're going to need the kind of research available to you at the Crescent Hotel & Spa in Eureka Springs, Arkansas. Located in a place so haunted that it calls itself America's Halloween City, the Crescent Hotel & Spa is an 1886 Victorian that has rumors and legends about ghostly apparitions and a huge historical archive for guests to explore. The Crescent Hotel & Spa also offers ghost tours and spooky performances at its outdoor theatre.

CANADA'S MOST HAUNTED LOCATIONS

Canada has endless myths and legends, but here are a few of the country's most popular haunted spots.

When a hotel room is so haunted that the hotel erases it from guests' view, you know it's got something weird going on. That's what happened with room 873 at the Fairmont Banff Springs Hotel in Banff, Alberta, a room with such a dark past—it's rumored that a murder-suicide happened there—that the 1888 hotel sealed it off from the public. The story goes that so many guests reported hearing screams and seeing bloody handprints in the room that management virtually erased it from the hotel's history.

A lodging with an even darker past is the HI Ottawa Jail Hostel in Ottawa, Ontario. This jail opened in 1862 and had such harsh living conditions—its windows were open to the elements all year long—that many more prisoners perished there than were executed in the prison's gallows (which you can still see if you take a tour). You can sleep in a tiny cell with bars for a door, or a regular room above the guards' quarters.

The ultimate vacation gone wrong—the voyage of the RMS *Titanic*—has left its impression in Halifax, Nova Scotia, where the remains of many of the ship's passengers were taken after being recovered. The Five Fisherman is a restaurant in Halifax. The building dates back to 1817. In April 1912 it served as the town's mortuary, and it is where some of the *Titanic*'s most famous passengers, like John Jacob Astor IV, were kept prior to burial. Employees report glasses flying off shelves, taps turning themselves on, and ghostly a maître d' appearing on the stairs.

GETTING READY TO HIT THE ROAD

Now that you've gotten a tiny sliver of North America's most notoriously haunted spots, the wheels must be turning about where to visit first. Wherever you choose to explore, make sure you've done your prep work first—not just doing research on the places and planning your routes, but also practicing your investigation techniques at home, or places near home, before you embark on a big, spooky trip. ■

The imposing walls of Fort Knox have glowered down at the Penobscot River for nearly two centuries.

PROSPECT, MAINE

FORT KNOX

Located on the western bank of the Penobscot River, this military garrison has been standing for more than 150 years and is rich in American and paranormal history

NAMED FOR MAJOR GENERAL HENRY KNOX (AMERICA'S FIRST SECRETARY of War) and designed by chief engineer Joseph Totten, Fort Knox remains one of the best-preserved examples of coastal defense fortifications constructed in the mid-1800s. The facility was originally built to protect the region against a possible future attack from the British navy. Troops, mostly volunteers undergoing training before being sent to active duty, were first garrisoned there from 1863 to 1866. The site also housed soldiers during the Spanish-American War in 1898, though the facility never became involved in military action.

Nevertheless, some of the troops who were summoned to the fort have never left. To this day, the spirits of former residents can be heard marching there, continuing to carry out their duties despite having departed from the earthly plane. "This would definitely be a more benign, fun, historic haunt," explains Amy, who along with her partner in the paranormal, Adam, investigated the activity at Fort Knox in the dead of winter back in 2011.

"We were just investigating to confirm hauntings at that time, so we were going anywhere that was remotely haunted," Amy says. "We were checking it out. There was really no end game for each place; it was just confirming whether it was actually haunted. So, that was pretty fun sometimes."

AMY BRUNI: The shadow figures there are pretty famous. I think that happens at a lot of forts, where you have soldiers who follow the same path constantly, day in and day out, doing their guard duties. They would take this certain path. So, I think [we were] seeing these soldiers still very much fulfilling their duties, walking back and forth and standing guard. I just remember it being very, very cold. It was like -12 or something, and we could only be outside for 20 minutes at a time.

ADAM BERRY: The fort was a block of ice. We're up in Maine. It's quiet. It's cold. It's on the water. It was so quiet because you don't hear footsteps on concrete—your sound is muffled by the snow that is literally caked all around you. So, when we would hear the voices—we would hear men talking at times—we knew that nobody was around. Sometimes, we can debunk or disprove something. [If] somebody's talking, we're like, "Oh, that sound is echoing from the other side of the fort. That's how sound travels." But because it was so quiet, when we heard something, it was almost like it was right next to us. I do remember hearing the voices of men talking

A former caretaker known as Leopold has often been reported patrolling the stone corridors (above). In the snowy silence, Adam and Amy heard voices near the walls (opposite bottom).

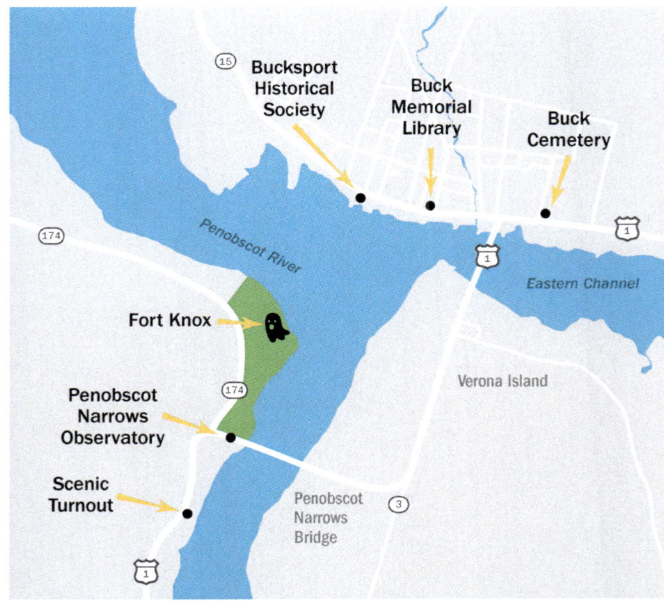

in the area where they kept the gunpowder, I think, and then seeing these shadow figures. We could sit there in that hallway, and watch these shadow figures walk back and forth all night long. They weren't interacting with us. Like Amy said, they were doing their duties still. It was a big residual haunt in terms of interaction.

AMY BRUNI: There was one apparition that's really interesting, the sergeant. His name was Leopold—he served as the sole caretaker of the fort all by himself for 13 years. A lot of people think that he's still patrolling. They describe his outfit and everything. He's still making sure that the fort is taken care of. He was there from 1887 to 1900.

ADAM BERRY: [My husband] Ben and I, we go up to Camden [Maine] a lot. The last time we were there, we just kept driving north to see what we could see. I realized that I was next to the fort. So, we pulled over, and there was a guy working there—it wasn't open to the public. This is in November. I talked to him for a minute, and I was like, "Yeah, we did a case here one time." He knew exactly who we were, and he started going on, [saying that the activity] "hasn't stopped." He's like, "They're my buddies." It was this old man, too. He had to be in his 70s. The groundskeeper is what I would call him. He was saying, "Yeah, they're my friends. Come back anytime you want, because they're still just patrolling and doing their duty." I mean, maybe he was a ghost? Was he real? He did let us in the bathroom, so maybe he's not a ghost. But he was definitely aware of our time there, and he was not shy about talking about how the experiences are still going on. I think they're going to be open to the public this summer, thankfully, because it is a beautiful historic place. ■

Fire claimed the resort twice before this lithograph was made in 1927.

EXCELSIOR SPRINGS, MISSOURI

THE ELMS HOTEL & SPA

From healing spring to mob hangout to modern luxury hotel, there is a lot of lively history in the halls of this resort

BACK IN 1880, WITH HIS DAUGHTER OPAL SUFFERING FROM INCURABLE tuberculosis, Missouri farmer Travis Mellion began inquiring after any remedy that could possibly help his ailing child. Eventually, he was brought some water from the nearby river, and sure enough, once Opal bathed in and drank from the spring water, her condition began to improve. When word got out that the girl had made a full recovery, it didn't take long for dozens of other families to descend on the site. Soon, the town of Excelsior Springs was born; a short time later, in 1888, The Elms Hotel & Spa opened for business.

In the days since, the property has seen both prosperity and hardship. The resort has hosted luminaries, including Harry S. Truman, but it's also been destroyed by fire twice, once in 1898 and then again in 1910. It's fallen into bankruptcy, only to be rescued and refurbished—most recently benefiting from a $20 million upgrade in 2011.

For a site so rich in history, it's perhaps not surprising that various ghosts and other entities have taken up residence at The Elms. But the resort embraces its reputation as a place not only for rest and relaxation but also for interdimensional interaction—aspiring ghost hunters should be advised to reserve the hotel's "paranormal package" for their stay.

AMY BRUNI: It's a very beautiful hotel. I guess the story goes that the springs it was built on in that area were considered healing waters. Now, there's a big lap pool in the basement, but that used to be a speakeasy. Apparently, some people died in the speakeasy, and so the pool itself is haunted.

ADAM BERRY: When we were on the fourth floor, we encountered the mimic in that hallway.

AMY BRUNI: We had some equipment that made very specific and distinct beeping sounds to alert us if there was some sort of EMF spike or temperature change. It was literally in our hands, and it was making some noises. Then we heard the exact same noises happen down the hallway. So, we go down there. Obviously, it's just us on that floor. We heard the sounds again down at the other end of the hallway. So, this thing was mimicking the sound of our equipment to us. Then I heard, right in my ear, this really loud sigh. I was freaked out. I thought, "Oh my God." I don't like disembodied voices at all, and this was literally in my ear. We caught it on our recorder and on camera. You could hear it. It was really loud. That top floor is super creepy.

ADAM BERRY: You know me, girl. I moved my room up there. I was the only person staying on that floor. They weren't renting those rooms out, but because we were filming there, they let me move up to one of those rooms. That was pretty creepy. I would sit in the living room area [of my suite], and I would watch the hallway light, just waiting for something to block out that light or pass by. I was being all badass, but I did not anticipate how I would feel doing that. I remember hearing weird noises at night, like somebody was in the hallway but nobody was there. They also

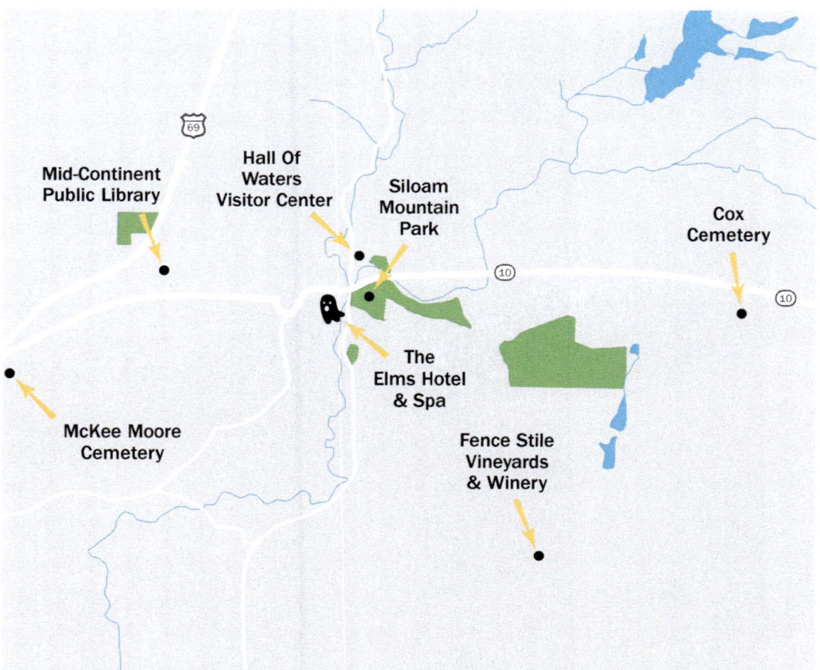

The waters of Excelsior Springs' river were thought to have healing properties (above). Sometimes long hallways cause strange echoes. Sometimes something else causes those sounds (opposite).

turned off the hallway lights on the main part [of the floor since] nobody was staying there—they were conserving energy. To walk out in the hallway and have it be pitch black was really weird.

After that experience [with the mimic], I thought that we were dealing with something that was playing tricks on us. We encounter that every so often. There's a theory that it can be associated with the land itself, some spiritual, maybe a Native American being that's connected to the land. Every once in a while, we'll encounter something that's nature-based, what we call elementals. I felt like that's what we were dealing with. It was something that was being a trickster, that wasn't necessarily a human entity, but something that was feeling us out and we were feeling it out. It was mimicking our equipment. It was breathing in Amy's ear and scaring her and walking around outside in the hallway when I was trying to sleep. I feel like it was sniffing us out just as much as we were sniffing it out.

AMY BRUNI: The Elms has a very strong history, supposedly, of mob [activity] back in the speakeasy days. Supposedly, Al Capone stayed there, but if I gave you a dollar for every place I've investigated where Al Capone supposedly hung out . . . He's like the woman in white. Everywhere I go, Al Capone or George Washington went there. But [allegedly] there were some murders on site that involved the mob. More than one man was killed by the mob in the basement area. So, it could be an elemental, or it could be the mob still hanging out, having a party. Who knows? But it's a cool place to visit, and we had some really neat experiences there. ▪

Something terrible is alleged to have happened in one of the tower rooms of this historic castle.

PORT TOWNSEND, WASHINGTON

MANRESA CASTLE

Forty miles outside of Seattle on the Quimper Peninsula stands an elegant, imposing home turned holy building turned hotel

THIS HISTORIC STRUCTURE WAS BUILT IN 1892 AS THE IMPRESSIVE residence of Charles and Kate Eisenbeis—Charles Eisenbeis served as the first mayor of Port Townsend, and he wanted a home reminiscent of the castles found in the couple's native Prussia. In the wake of Charles' death in 1902 and Kate's subsequent remarriage, however, the grand, 4-story, 30-room building was left vacant, with only a single caretaker to look after it. Over time, the castle became a getaway for nuns and then a training facility for priests before it was transformed into a hotel in 1968.

As is so often the case with a building this old, ghosts of the past reportedly linger at the site. Visitors have described encountering both a monk, who is believed to have taken his own life after suffering a crisis of faith, and a young woman, who reportedly threw herself from a third-floor window when her lover was feared to have been lost at sea. When Amy and Adam visited Manresa Castle with psychic medium Chip Coffey, they encountered a range of paranormal activity, even making contact with the spirit of the departed monk.

AMY BRUNI: Manresa Castle was completed 1892. [Later] a Seattle attorney bought the castle as a vacation place for nuns teaching in Seattle schools. That didn't work out. In 1927, the Jesuit priests purchased the building as a college. The priests spent their final year of training there, studying ascetic theology. They added a large wing housing a chapel and sleeping rooms in 1928. The Jesuits left it in 1968, but supposedly there was a pretty well-known suicide that happened there in one of the tower rooms. There was a monk who hanged himself in one of the rooms upstairs, the circle room, and that is who they think haunts the place. Now, it's a hotel.

ADAM BERRY: We were there a full day [and night] before everyone else showed up [for this event we were hosting]. Most of the time when you stay at a hotel, you're not going to notice the ghosts if they're there because there's so many people walking around. When no one is there, it turns into *The Shining*.

AMY BRUNI: I had a very creepy experience there with my daughter. We were there for this event, and my daughter was really sick. I had to take her to the ER; she had a crazy

Amy and Adam had to take a ferry across the chilly waters of Port Townsend Bay (above) to reach the elegant and eerie castle (opposite).

fever. She was in bed, asleep. [In the] morning, one of our attendees came up to me [during breakfast], and she was like, "Charlotte sure was up late last night. I heard her running up and down the hallway, giggling." I was like, "Actually, Charlotte's been throwing up for the last 24 hours." There were no [other] kids in the whole building.

ADAM BERRY: [When] Chip arrived, we were sitting in that room that has the chandelier where supposedly the guy hanged himself. It's like the air was very thick and made us feel uneasy. We experience that occasionally when an entity is trying its best to make us not be there. We can always tell. It feels weird; something is not right. I remember interacting with [an entity] we thought was the person that committed suicide. We were using the SLS camera, which maps a body. It's a camera that, basically, when you point it in a direction, sometimes a stick figure will come up. The theory is that it's mapping what you cannot see. We've had [these figures] interact with us and wave at us. [Here,] our equipment was going off, and it was answering questions. He definitely reached out to us. It felt sad, like he had something to say. I don't think many people investigate that place. It was the first time that we were able to connect with this spirit who needed closure.

AMY BRUNI: It's on our list [to revisit].

ADAM BERRY: We deal with a lot of different entities, and sometimes you don't know who you're going to be talking to. You have an idea, but you don't know who it is or why they're there. You don't know what they were going through the moments before they died, or if they had a hand in their own death. You want to be sympathetic to that because if they're still there, they have a story to be told. ▪

Guests, soldiers and crewman have been walking the decks of the *Queen Mary* since 1936.

LONG BEACH, CALIFORNIA

THE *QUEEN MARY*

By turns a luxury cruise ship and a troop transport, this ocean liner has some stories to tell

WHEN THE *QUEEN MARY* DEPARTED FROM SOUTHAMPTON, ENGLAND, for her maiden voyage on May 27, 1936, the British luxury ocean liner was every inch the epitome of seafaring elegance. Designed to appeal to society's wealthiest echelons, the ship boasted multiple dining rooms, cocktail bars, swimming pools, squash courts and even a small hospital. Yet during the Second World War, her size and speed were put to a different use—painted camouflage gray, she was stripped of her sumptuous trappings to serve as a troop transport. By the time the war ended, the ship, redubbed the *Grey Ghost*, had carried a total of 810,000 military personnel, though not all of them survived their journeys.

"It was used during World War II to bring soldiers home," explains Amy. "She could get soldiers and bring them back really quickly and basically outmaneuver radar and other ships. But they took some injured troops on board, and then people passed. Once the war was over, they refitted her with all her luxury accoutrements, and life went on."

Restored to her former glory, the *Queen Mary* resumed transatlantic passenger service from 1947–1967, when she docked in Long Beach, California, for the final time. But the ship, which now serves as a hotel and a popular wedding destination, has continued to be an object of fascination over the decades—especially among those with an interest in the paranormal.

AMY BRUNI: The *Queen Mary*—it's so bizarre because it just feels haunted. I mean, we've been to a lot of very haunted places, but you walk on there and you're like, "Ooh, this doesn't feel right."

ADAM BERRY: There's a theory that running water is a conduit for energy. If you have a ship sitting in a harbor where the constant tides are going in and out, water is moving, there could be something to it that makes it a little bit more active than other locations in the country.

AMY BRUNI: There is a very famous ghost of a little girl in the pool room, who is very chatty and has been seen a number of times. I saw in the boiler room probably one of the strangest apparitions I've ever seen in my life. Now, the boiler room is completely set up with walkways and things, so it's very safe, and they do tours down there. At this time, no one was really allowed down there—they were giving us special access to do this event. I was down there with my friend, and we were walking around. All we had were our flashlights. I put my flashlight up to look around, and I see this man walk by—but not the whole man. It was the top part of his torso. I saw his shoulder and his arm down to his hip on one side and half his head, and he was wearing canvas overalls. I could literally see the sweat on his head. It was so bizarre. My friend was staring in the same exact direction. I asked, "Did you just see that?" And he's like, "Yeah. What was that?" I mean, this was a big guy, and then just gone. Clearly a ghost. So, then I found out—I was not aware of it at the time—supposedly there's a very famous ghost in the boiler room. His name is John Henry. We saw exactly what people have been reporting down there for years.

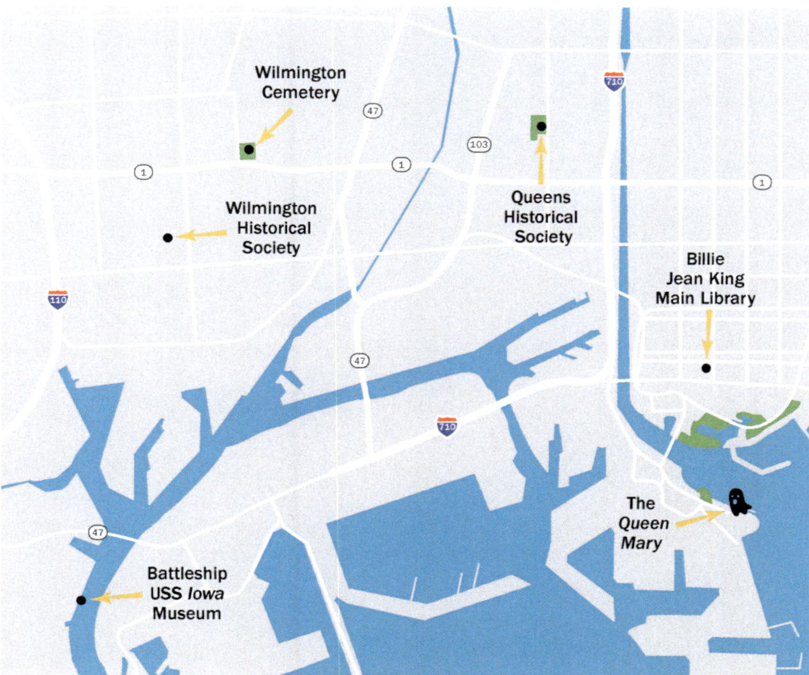

The smokestacks have stopped puffing since the ship became a permanently docked hotel (opposite). You can take guided ghost tours of the ship, which include infamously active locations like the pool (above).

ADAM BERRY: The front part of the ship, just past room B340, there's a doorway that goes deeper into the forward part of the ship. Supposedly, people, [possibly] prisoners, were chained in that area, [and an] accident happened [that] caused the death of those prisoners inside that space. We've gotten interesting EVPs in that space—just acknowledging that they're in the space still. I find it interesting that when we investigate, we find that ghosts and spirits sometimes go to the least populated areas to get away from us [humans]—like the basement or the attic in a house. They're going to go and do their thing. So, you have to go and find them. . . . For these bigger locations, there are other teams that investigate, so [the information that's collected is] like a case study—this is our experience at this place, and this is what we found. Then other investigators go and investigate. It builds this whole portfolio of activity for a location.

AMY BRUNI: We share whenever we can. Some of the things we really are big proponents for in the paranormal are sharing not only your investigation results but also your research, your theories and your ideas. For a minute, the paranormal field was falling into this very streamlined way of thinking. We really started thinking outside the box and that has affected the way these cases are researched across the board.

ADAM BERRY: We are open books in terms of the experiences that we've had, because our experiences are different than others. Just putting it all together is a puzzle anyway. ■

Unbelievable as some of them seem, most campfire tales have at least a kernel of truth in them.

THE WORLD'S SPOOKIEST TRUE TALES

No matter where you travel, you're sure to find ghost stories. Some are from the modern day and others are from ancient times, but they're all sure to give you the chills.

By Gina McIntyre

THE JERSEY DEVIL

This is one of America's oldest enduring legends: When, in 1735, an Estellville, New Jersey, resident known as Mother Leeds learned she was expecting her thirteenth child, she uttered in despair, "Let it be the devil." To her great horror, her wish came true. The unwanted infant transformed at birth into a hideous monster with horns, claws and wings. The creature flew away into the vast forests of the Pine Barrens, where it has roamed ever since. Curiously, although he was unwanted by his parents, the Devil has subsequently been embraced by his home state. He became New Jersey's official "state demon" in 1938 and is the namesake of the local National Hockey League franchise. The Devil also has been immortalized in popular culture, film, music and on television, including in an early episode of the spooky television series *The X-Files*.

LA LLORONA

Well known throughout Latin America, Mexico's La Llorona is, like so many legends, rooted in a tale of tragedy. Upon learning of her husband's infidelity, a distraught woman drowns her two children in an ill-conceived act of revenge. Immediately overwhelmed with guilt and regret, she takes her own life yet is condemned to wander the earth searching for her lost little ones. Usually glimpsed near bodies of water, the wailing woman appears dressed in white, eternally in mourning—seeking to claim any children as she desperately searches for her own. (In some version of the tale, she seeks out male victims). The story, which has inspired several films, most recently 2019's Guatemalan supernatural horror drama *La Llorona*, serves as a powerful reminder to young listeners to stick close to home after dark.

RESURRECTION MARY

Just south of Chicago in Justice, Illinois, along a stretch of Archer Avenue, a young woman dressed in white walks the roadway alone. Should a kind passerby stop and offer to drive her to her destination, she will accept politely and remain seated quietly—until the car nears Resurrection Cemetery. At which point, the passenger will become animated and insist that she be let out. She'll quickly exit the vehicle and disappear behind the cemetery's iron gates. "Resurrection Mary," as the ghost has come to be known, has been sighted since the 1930s when a man first claimed to have met the winning young lady at the Oh Henry Ballroom, where they spent the evening dancing together. As he was driving her home, she insisted that she be let out at the cemetery, and then vanished. In the years since, panicked drivers will, from time to time, report having hit a slim blonde woman with their car—yet when they stop to try to help her, they're unable to find a body.

THE BELL WITCH

Shortly after John Bell moved his family to a 300-acre holding near modern-day Adams, Tennessee, in 1804, he observed a creature with the body of a dog and the head of a rabbit while working in the fields. It was only the first of a series of increasingly unsettling visitations for the clan, who found themselves relentlessly tormented and attacked by an unseen entity. John's daughter Betsy was left with welts and bruises on her body from the assaults. The disturbances were all courtesy of a spirit that became known as the Bell Witch, believed to be the ghost of Bell's neighbor Kate Batts. The violent presence was simply vicious toward the family—when John Bell died after becoming unconscious, a vial of poison was reportedly discovered in the home, having been planted there by none other than the malicious entity. So many decades later, the Bell property remains famous for paranormal activity with numerous reports of inexplicable lights and unsettling sounds emanating from the area—especially from a cave on the property.

BLOODY MARY

Stand before a mirror in a darkened room, chant the name Bloody Mary over and over and soon a ghastly image of a woman will appear positioned ominously behind you in the reflection. The parlor game has frightened teenagers at slumber parties for decades, but the legend has terrifying real-world roots. The woman in the mirror is most commonly thought to be the ghost of a witch named Mary Worth, who allegedly abducted and mutilated runaway slaves around the time of the American Civil War. She was eventually tied to a stake by the local citizenry and burned to death. (The name Bloody Mary is, however, also associated with Mary I, who reigned as queen of England from 1553 until her death in 1558.) Interestingly, Japan has its own answer to the ghastly apparition: Hanako-san, a spirit that haunts girls' school bathrooms. South Africa, too, boasts its own corollary—the pink-haired demon Pinky Pinky.

THE BROWN LADY OF RAYNHAM HALL

The subject of one of the most well-known spectral photographs ever taken, the Brown Lady, haunts Norfolk, England's Raynham Hall, a historic manor that dates to the 17th century. She is believed to be the ghost of Lady Dorothy Townshend née Walpole, wife of Lord Charles Townshend and sister of Britain's first prime minister, Robert Walpole. Sadly, the Townshends' union was reported to be unhappy and contentious. Dorothy was eventually confined to her rooms at their Norfolk estate before her death on March 29, 1726, at age 40, possibly from smallpox. The apparition has been glimpsed many times throughout the years, always dressed in a brown, brocade gown. Her likeness was captured on film in 1936, when photographers from *Country Life* magazine witnessed the ghost descending the central staircase.

GJENGANGER

Violent and vengeful, Scandinavia's gjenganger is unique in the spirit world. Often taking corporeal form, this is an entity that has returned from the grave seeking to attack those who wronged it in life (gjenganger literally translates as "walking after death"). This type of being dates to Viking times, when it was widely held that a pinch from one of the creatures could prove fatal, and burial rituals were altered to prevent the recently deceased—typically, people who had committed suicide or had been murdered—from returning. Most often, inscriptions were made inside of the coffin to ensure the corpse would not become a gjenganger.

TUNNELTON, INDIANA

About an hour south of the sprawling Bloomington campus of Indiana University lies the small, unincorporated town of Tunnelton, Indiana, fittingly named for a series of railroad tunnels running through the region. Originally constructed in 1857, the largest of them—the Big Tunnel—spans a third of a mile and ranks as one of the Midwest state's most haunted places. Numerous sightings of ghosts have taken place there over the years, but one of the most famous is believed to be the spirit of Henry Dixon. According to reports, after Dixon was murdered, his body was brought to the tunnel, his killer believing that passing trains would destroy Dixon's remains and eliminate any incriminating evidence. Indeed, the perpetrator of the crime was never caught, leaving Dixon to wander the tunnel at night, eternally seeking justice.

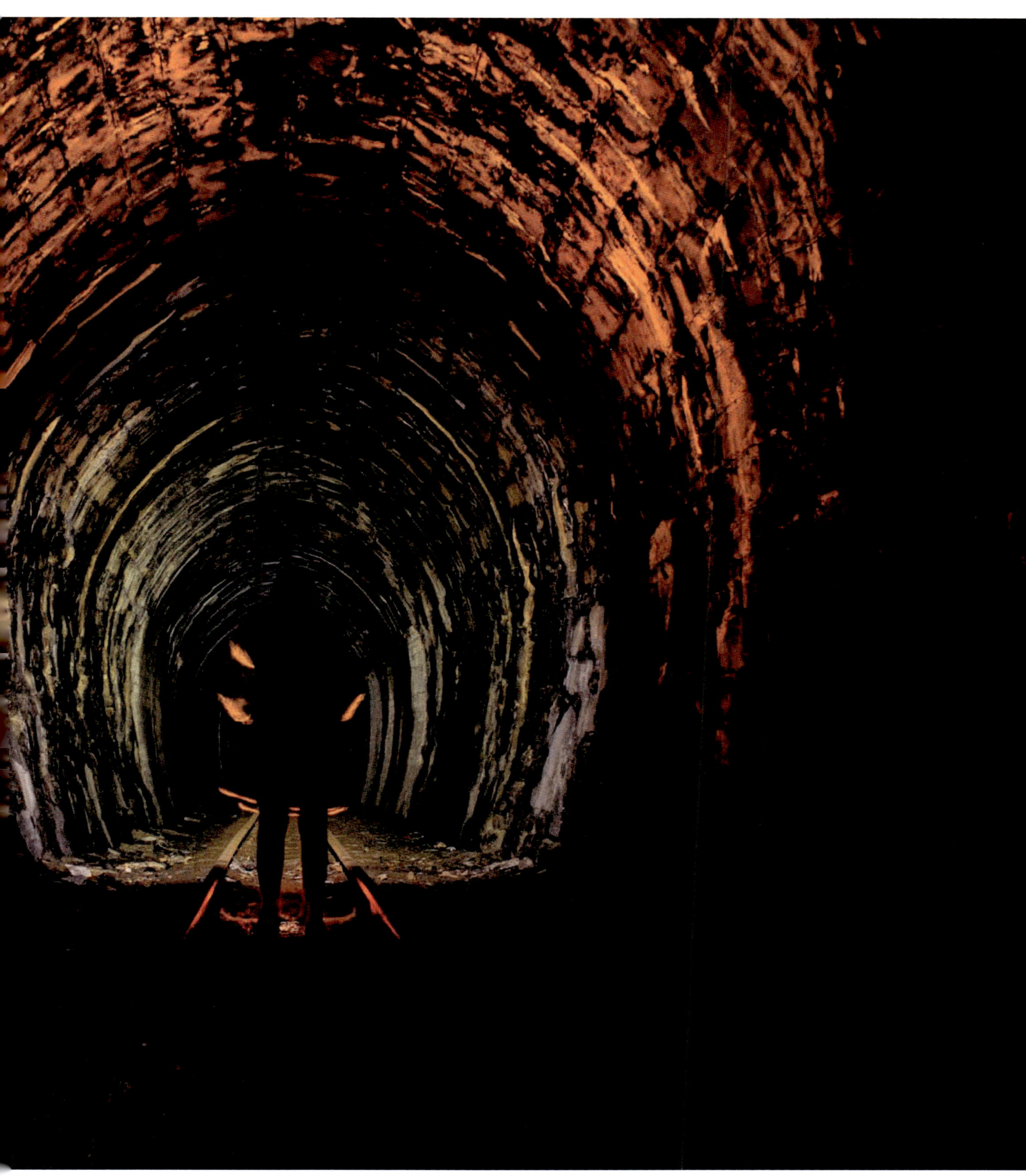

THE NIGHT MARCHERS

Roaming across the Hawaiian Islands is a band of ancient spirit warriors known as the Night Marchers. Their arrival is heralded by the sounds of drums, chanting and blasts from a conch shell. The ghosts carry torches to illuminate their path, and they've been known to traverse open expanses and to move through buildings, all in ceremonial formation. They're most often found during the last four moon phases at sites including O'ahu's Makaha Valley Plantation and Ka'ena Point and Kalama Valley. As the Night Marchers pass, any onlookers must take care not to draw their gaze, as the high-ranking chiefs are so sacred that mortals are not permitted to look upon them under threat of death. Witnesses are urged to crouch low to the ground and avert their eyes—and even urinate—as signs of submissiveness.

KRAMPUS

A nightmarish figure from Alpine folklore, Krampus is a half man, half goat who arrives every December to beat misbehaving children with birch sticks, or worse, to stuff them into his satchel and drag them off to hell—think Satan rather than Santa. A dark counterpoint to kindly St. Nicholas, the horned creature with the cloven hoofs is thought to be the son of Hel, the Norse god of the underworld. He takes center stage on December 5, when Austrian men sprint through the streets dressed as the mythic beast for the ritual of *Krampuslauf* ("Krampus run"). Much like the Jersey Devil, Krampus has developed an unlikely fan following, even inspiring a 2015 satirical horror comedy that bears his name.

HENRY CLAY

THE PHANTOM STEAMBOAT *ELIZA BATTLE*

On March 1, 1858, a 315-ton paddlewheel steamboat named the *Eliza Battle* was making its way south on a stretch of the Tombigbee River toward Mobile, Alabama, carrying more than 1,200 bales of cotton on its deck when a fire broke out. Miles from the capital and with the blaze quickly growing out of control, the 60 desperate passengers aboard the vessel—along with 45 crewmen—were forced to leap into the icy waters as they abandoned ship. Although some survived by clinging to trees along the waterway until they could be rescued, more than 30 people perished. Today, the ghostly ship rests at the bottom of the Tombigbee River, and the terrified screams of the dead can be heard calling in vain for help from the water.

WATER BABIES

Among many of the indigenous peoples of the western United States, there exists a legend about dangerous water spirits who take the form of infants, some with fish tails or gills, their cries luring unsuspecting victims to their death. The tales of these water babies vary from tribe to tribe and region to region. In Nevada, for example, water babies are thought to be ill-formed or premature infants who were laid to rest into Pyramid Lake by the Paiute tribe. In Utah, however, the Ute people warned of underwater dwarves who would mimic the sounds of babies in distress, only to drag anyone who ventured too close into the depths of Utah Lake. No matter what shape these tales take, though, the one constant is the distressing cries of ghostly children.

GHOST HUNTING
Editorial Director Kostya Kennedy
Senior Editor Alyssa Smith
Design, Photo, and Copy Tandem Books, Inc.
Writers Gina McIntyre, Julie Tremaine
Reporter Daniel S. Levy
Premedia Trafficking Supervisor Tony Jungweber
Color Quality Analyst John Santucci

MEREDITH PREMIUM PUBLISHING
Vice President & Group Publisher Scott Mortimer
Vice President, Group Editorial Director Stephen Orr
Vice President, Marketing Jeremy Biloon
Executive Publishing Director Megan Pearlman
Director, Brand Marketing Jean Kennedy
Associate Director, Brand Marketing Bryan Christian
Senior Brand Manager Katherine Barnet
Associate Director, Business Development and Partnerships Nina Reed

Editorial Director Kostya Kennedy
Creative Director Gary Stewart
Director of Photography Christina Lieberman
Senior Editor Alyssa Smith
Editorial Operations Director Jamie Roth Major
Manager, Editorial Operations Gina Scauzillo
Special thanks Brad Beatson, Samantha Lebofsky, Kate Roncinske, Laura Villano

MEREDITH NATIONAL MEDIA GROUP
President Catherine Levene
President, Meredith Magazines Doug Olson
President, Consumer Products Tom Witschi
President, Meredith Digital Alysia Borsa
EVP, Strategic & Business Development Daphne Kwon

EXECUTIVE VICE PRESIDENTS
Chief Revenue Officer Michael Brownstein
Digital Sales Marla Newman
Finance Michael Riggs
Marketing & Integrated Communications Nancy Weber

SENIOR VICE PRESIDENTS
Consumer Marketing Steve Crowe
Consumer Revenue Andy Wilson
Corporate Sales Brian Kightlinger
Foundry 360 Matt Petersen
Product & Technology Justin Law
Research Solutions Britta Cleveland
Strategic Planning Amy Third
Strategic Sourcing, Newsstand, Production Chuck Howell

VICE PRESIDENTS
Brand Licensing Toye Cody and Sondra Newkirk
Business Planning & Analysis Rob Silverstone
Corporate Communications Jill Davison
Finance Chris Susil
Strategic Development Kelsey Andersen
Strategic Partnerships Alicia Cervini

Vice President, Group Editorial Director Stephen Orr
Chief Digital Content Officer Amanda Dameron
Director, Editorial Operations & Finance Greg Kayko

MEREDITH CORPORATION
Chairman & Chief Executive Officer Tom Harty
Chief Financial Officer Jason Frierott
Chief Development Officer John Zieser
President, Meredith Local Media Group Patrick McCreery
Senior Vice President, Human Resources Dina Nathanson
Senior Vice President, Chief Communications Officer Erica Jensen

Vice Chairman Mell Meredith Frazier

TANDEM BOOKS INC.
www.tandem-books.com
Creative Director Ashley Prine
Editorial Director Katherine Furman

PRINTED IN THE USA

PICTURE CREDITS
Front cover: Matthew Troke/Shutterstock
Back cover: courtesy of the authors
Inside front/inside back covers: LordRunar/iStockphoto/Getty Images

Page numbers in **bold**

Courtesy of the authors: **4**, **18**, **20**, **21**, **22**, **23**, **40**, **42**, **43**, **47**, **65**
Courtesy of Michael Beck: **24**, **26**, **27**
Maps provided by Tandem Books: **23**, **27**, **39**, **43**, **47**, **51**, **65**, **69**, **73**, **77**
Courtesy of Ben Berry: **76**
© savoryexposure/flickr: **50**

Shutterstock: **1** © dik az; **2** © TomasHrivnak; **5**, **19**, **25**, **37**, **41**, **45**, **49**, **63**, **67**, **71**, **75** © Stephanie Frey; **6** © zef art; **8** © Ingaav; **11** © Skreidzeleu; **12** © Marti Bug Catcher; **13** © Vladimir Mulder; **14** © 2021 Photography; **28** © Francey; **30** © OtmarW; **33** © elebeZoom; **35** (bottom) © Ines19; **36** © KLiK Photography; **38** © Angela N Perryman; **39** © Binh Dong; **46** © Jimmy Rooney; **51** © Billy F Blume Jr; **52** © Jarno Holappa; **57** © ehrlif; **58** © Juiced Up Media; **59** © William Cushman; **64** © Zack Frank; **78** © Johnny Adolphson; **80** © poidl; **83** © Raggedstone; **84** © Wayne Hsieh78; **87** © Romolo Tavani; **89** © Damian Pankowiec; **91** © Nicola Simeoni; **94** © Jakub Krechowicz

Getty Images: **10** © Palani Mohan/Fairfax Media; **16** © Sepia Times/Universal Images Group; **17** © joegolby/iStock /Getty Images Plus; **31**, **81** © urbazon; **32** © Bob Bernier; **34** © Science & Society Picture Library; **35** (top) © David Wall; **44** © Carol M. Highsmith/Buyenlarge; **54** © Joe Raedle; **55** © Jim Davis/The Boston Globe; **56** © Alfred Eisenstaedt/The LIFE Picture Collection; **60** © C Flanigan; **61** © George Rose; **62** © The Print Collector; **66** © Smith Collection/Gado; **73** © coutesy of the authors; **74** © Topical Press Agency; **77** © ris Schneider/Los Angeles Times; **81** © urbazon; **85** © D-Keine; **90** © RonTech2000; **92** © Heritage Art/Heritage Images; **96** © Matthew Jonas/MediaNews Group/Boulder Daily Camera

Alamy Stock Photo: **48** © Moviestore Collection Ltd ; **70** © George Ostertag; **86** © Smith Archive

THE STANLEY HOTEL IN ESTES PARK, COLORADO
Visit the spirited hotel that inspired Stephen King's *The Shining* on page 59.